JESUS
IS FOR EVERYONE

A SOURCE BOOK
FOR CHURCH SERVICES

John C Sharp & John Wilson

SAINT ANDREW PRESS

First published in 1992 by
SAINT ANDREW PRESS
121 George Street
Edinburgh EH2 4YN

Copyright © John C Sharp & John Wilson 1992

ISBN 0 7152 0649 4

British Library in Cataloguing Data

A catalogue record for this book
is available from the British Library.

0-7512-0649-4

Typeset in Palatino.

Printed and bound by Bell and Bain Ltd, Glasgow.

*The Publisher acknowledges
financial assistance from
The Drummond Trust
towards the publication of this volume.*

Contents

To two Patient Wives—
Allison and Jean

Introduction

This book of scripts originated from a desire to communicate Christian concerns in a fresh way. It develops some of the ideas contained in our first book, *Life is for Everyone* (also available from Saint Andrew Press). We have called this volume of scripts *Jesus is for Everyone* because that is true, and it seems to us to reflect the ethos of many of the individual items.

These new scripts have been worked out in services of worship and other group situations over a number of years. They are designed for use in a variety of settings and include interviews, letters, dialogues, stories and testimonies. They are instructive, challenging, encouraging; some are satirical.

The interviews and letters feature biblical, or imaginary people. They deal with biblical events or contemporary situations. The dialogues seek to explore aspects of Christian belief and practice. The stories are types of parables to illustrate some modern attitudes and biblical truths. The Testimonies illustrate various viewpoints and experiences.

This book is divided into three main sections: 'The Christian Year', 'The Life of the Church' and 'The Life of the Christian'. This will make it easy to select suitable scripts.

Scripts can be used:

— to illuminate a sermon point;
— outwith the sermon to illustrate a specific theme;
— together to make a composite programme: *eg* Easter;
— in various meetings: youth, women's, men's *etc*;
— as part of an epilogue;
— as discussion starters;
— for school assemblies.

The book itself may be useful for dipping into and as a source of interest, encouragement or challenge. The use of the book is limited only by the imagination of the user.

These scripts are sent out in the prayerful hope that they will be used by God to bring comfort and challenge.

John C Sharp & John Wilson 1992

About the Authors

JOHN C SHARP BSc, BD, PhD began his career in the Steel Industry, but left to train for the Ministry. He subsequently gained a doctorate in the field of Science and Religion. He is currently Chairman of the Board of Directors of the National Bible Society of Scotland and is Minister for East Kilbride South.

JOHN WILSON BA also worked in the Steel industry for many years, but accepted redundancy in 1976 to devote time to freelance writing. He is currently a Vice-President of the National Bible Society of Scotland and is both an Elder and Reader in the Church of Scotland.

The book *Jesus is for Everyone* is the second volume of resource material by the same authors. The first volume—*Life is for Everyone*—has proved very popular and is still available from Saint Andrew Press.

Part I
THE CHRISTIAN YEAR

Christmas

1 INTERVIEW—Isaiah

INTERVIEWER: Isaiah was one of the great prophets who looked forward to the deliverance of God.

Isaiah, you are a prophet of the Lord. Often you give us hints that One will come. A Deliverer. A Redeemer. Can you tell us about him?

ISAIAH: He will come.

INTERVIEWER: Will he descend from heaven with chariots of fire and with all the power of the Lord?

ISAIAH: I don't think so. It will be quiet. It will be strange. A virgin shall conceive and give birth to a son. And he will be called Immanuel—God with us.

INTERVIEWER: You mean God's promised One will come as a baby?

ISAIAH: Yes, although I cannot see it clearly. But a child will be born. A son will be given.

INTERVIEWER: So God will send—just a baby!

ISAIAH: Yes! But the government will be on his shoulders. And he will be called Wonderful Counsellor, the Mighty God, the Everlasting Father, the Prince of Peace.

INTERVIEWER: And this baby will grow up to be a great king?

ISAIAH: Yes, he will reign on the throne of David forever. Of the increase of his government, and of peace, there will be no end.

INTERVIEWER: Will he be armed with the power of the angels and of the Lord? Will he be able to slay our foes and lift our nation high?

ISAIAH: No, I don't think so. I don't really know.

INTERVIEWER: But surely, as the one from God, he will crush the evil ones and slay the wicked.

ISAIAH: Perhaps he will be crushed first.

INTERVIEWER: What do you mean?

ISAIAH: I know—and yet I don't know. It's not clear. Yes, he will be a servant of the Lord of Glory. Indeed he will *be* the Lord of Glory. But—somehow—I see a suffering servant.

INTERVIEWER: A suffering servant! God's promised One! How can that be?

ISAIAH: God's thoughts are not our thoughts; neither are his ways our ways.

INTERVIEWER: But the people—*God's* people—they will rally to his defence. How can he suffer? They won't let him suffer.

ISAIAH: I see him as despised and rejected of men. A man of deep sorrows, painfully familiar with suffering. No, I don't fully understand it, but he will have no beauty or majesty to attract us to him. He will be despised and rejected.

INTERVIEWER: You mean the coming king will be *despised* —by us?

ISAIAH: We will reject him. Indeed he will be stricken and afflicted by God.

INTERVIEWER: But why? I don't understand—how can such things be?

ISAIAH: I don't fully understand either. But, somehow or other, he will be pierced for our transgressions; crushed for our iniquities. Our peace will come through his punishment. It is by his wounds we will be healed.

INTERVIEWER: Are you saying that this coming King will suffer and die? That it will all end in failure?

ISAIAH: Failure? How can the Holy One of Israel, the Sovereign Lord, be defeated? He sits enthroned above the circle of the earth—its people are like grasshoppers in his sight. How can he fail?

INTERVIEWER: But what of the nation—how can you have a people with a dead king?

ISAIAH: I don't know the whole story and can't see the full picture clearly. But I do know that out of death there will be life; out of suffering there will be health; out of sorrow there will be everlasting joy; and out of shame will come eternal peace.

INTERVIEWER: But how?

ISAIAH: The zeal of the Lord will accomplish this. He will create a new heaven and a new earth. Evil will not be remembered and God will rejoice and take delight in his people. The sound of weeping and crying will be heard no more. The zeal of the Lord will bring all this to pass. I know not how it will come to be—but come it will. And it will come through the suffering servant of the Lord God Almighty.

2 STORY—The Wise Men

Behold there came wise men from the East saying, 'Where is he that is born King of the Jews? We have seen his star in the East and have come to worship him.'

And the people were greatly troubled, for they knew not what the wise men were saying. It was a time of great festivity in the land and the people were burdened with buying presents, spending money without thought. And they told the wise men to go and search elsewhere.

Then one of the wise men said, 'Behold a star!' And in the sky, high above the city roofs, a star twinkled and shone in a myriad of colours. So they hastened to where they had seen the star. Behold, when they came to the place where the star was resting, they found a great multitude gathered. There, in the bright lights that banished darkness, they saw the star.

But it was an electronic star on the top of a massive Christmas tree—decorated with tinsel, and lights that flickered and shone. With sadness in their hearts the wise men realised that it was not the star they had followed.

As they tried to talk one to another, lo they found it impossible. There was noise, and great was the sound thereof. Music, strange to their ears, thundered forth with a savage, syncopated beat. There was much singing and shouting and many wished them 'A Merry Christmas!' But the wise men did not understand it at all.

'Where is he that is born to be King?' they asked. The people only stared at them with bewilderment. They knew not of what they spake and could only laugh.

Then a young girl, bright-eyed, with a laughing countenance, said to them, 'Come with me.' They followed her with uplifted hearts. She seemed to know where the new born king was to be found.

But it was not so! She brought them to a policeman who stood near the great buildings that were floodlit, almost dazzling to the eye. 'These men have lost a child,' she said to the guardian of the law. And she vanished into the multitude with laughter and a song on her lips.

The policeman turned to the wise men. 'It wasn't wise bringing a child into a party this size. Or if you had to, then you should have held on to him tightly. Now, where did you last see him?' The policeman took a notebook from his pocket.

'But we have not yet seen him,' confessed one of the wise men. 'Lo, it came to pass that we saw his star in the East and have come to worship him.'

'Now, now, now,' smiled the policeman as he put his notebook back into his pocket. 'I know it's Christmas and maybe a little drink doesn't do anyone any harm. But I think you've had a little too much. So my advice is for you to go home and sleep it off. You shouldn't drink too much at your age.' And the policeman walked away from the place where the wise men stood.

With sadness in their hearts, the wise men hurried away from where the great multitude were celebrating Christmas. And they continued their search for the one who was born to be king.

3 INTERVIEW—Elizabeth

INTERVIEWER: Many were involved in the events of the first Christmas—Augustus Caesar, Zechariah and Elizabeth, Mary and Joseph, the shepherds and the wise men, Herod and Simeon. Suppose we could talk to some of them—what would they say?

Elizabeth, I believe you know Mary, the mother of Jesus?

ELIZABETH: Know her? Of course I know her, she's my cousin.

INTERVIEWER: Like Mary, you had rather an exciting experience before the birth of your son.

ELIZABETH: It was not just me, it was Zechariah also—he's my husband. In fact, it all began with him.

INTERVIEWER: What happened?

ELIZABETH: Well—my husband serves the Lord in the

Temple. One day, when all the congregation prayed out-side, he went in to burn incense before the Lord. He was alone—then suddenly, he was not alone. An angel came to him—Gabriel. He came with a message for Zechariah and me. A message from heaven *for us*.

INTERVIEWER: That's interesting! What was the message?

ELIZABETH: Our prayers had been heard and answered. God was going to give us a son. And this was to be no ordinary son.

INTERVIEWER: What do you mean, he was not to be ordinary?

ELIZABETH: We were to call him John—and there are no Johns in our family. But it was not just the name. He is to be great in the sight of the Lord. He is to be filled with the Holy Spirit from his birth. He is to go before the Lord in the spirit and power of Elijah. He is to be a forerunner —to prepare people for the Lord. He is to be a Prophet of the Most High.

INTERVIEWER: What did your husband think about that? What was his reaction?

ELIZABETH: He could hardly believe it. In fact he would *not* believe it. So the angel struck him dumb until the baby—our John—was born. It was a trying time. But you mentioned Mary. That was even more exciting. She came to see me—in my sixth month.

INTERVIEWER: Yes! I would like to know more about Mary. I believe you said she came to see you.

ELIZABETH: Yes! And her news was even more wonderful. She was expecting a child—but she was a virgin, you see! An angel had appeared to her also—and to Joseph, her betrothed. She was bearing a child who would be more than a prophet. He would be called the Son of the Most High. The Lord God would give him the throne of David and he would reign forever. His Kingdom would never end. I tell you the baby leapt within me when I heard Mary's news.

INTERVIEWER: All this seems incredible. What do you think it means?

ELIZABETH: It means our lives can never be the same again. Mary, Joseph, Zechariah, myself—nothing will ever be the same again. But it is not just we who are affected. The world will never be the same again.

INTERVIEWER: The world? What do you mean?

ELIZABETH: What do I mean? I don't understand it all. John and Jesus are just little babies. But we have been told by God that these are no ordinary children. John has come to be a Prophet. And Jesus is to be the One who will save us from our sins.

Yes, John will be a prophet. But Jesus—it is Jesus who will be the Saviour.

4 INTERVIEW—A Shepherd

INTERVIEWER: And it came to pass that Jesus was born in Bethlehem—and they laid him in a manger because there was no room for them in the inn. And there were shepherds abiding in the fields watching their flocks by night.

You are one of the shepherds who had rather a strange experience in the fields outside Bethlehem.

SHEPHERD: Strange. It was strange all right!

INTERVIEWER: Tell us what happened?

SHEPHERD: It began as an ordinary sort of night, routine —watching the sheep, looking out for wild animals, keeping the fire going, talking, you know the sort of thing. Then it happened! My mind still whirls when I think about it.

INTERVIEWER: Well, what happened?

SHEPHERD: An angel appeared to us!

INTERVIEWER: An angel? How did you know it was an angel?

SHEPHERD: How did we know? Have *you* ever seen an angel? I tell you, when you see an angel you know it's an angel. It's—he's—like nothing on earth (*laughs*)—that's a joke, isn't it? Angel—like nothing on earth! But it's no laughing matter. This angel—he was like no creature we had ever seen. He seemed all light—colour—beauty. We were terrified. *Awestruck!* Yes, that's the word—awestruck! And it was not just the angel. A light shone all around. It was indescribable.

INTERVIEWER: But what actually happened? Did this angel speak to you?

SHEPHERD: Yes, and do you know his first words? 'Don't be afraid.' He was gentle. Imagine, this angel was troubled because *he* frightened *us*. You don't expect to be treated with respect by an angel.

INTERVIEWER: That's interesting—but what else did this angel say to you? He must have said more than that!

SHEPHERD: Yes, I'm sorry. I get mixed up when I tell the story. It was all so strange. But I'll never forget his words. 'Don't be afraid,' he said, 'I bring you good news of great joy that will be for all the people. Today in the town of David, a Saviour has been born to you; he is Christ the Lord.'

INTERVIEWER: What do you think that meant?

SHEPHERD: It meant good news—just as the angel said. The Messiah—the Promised One of God had come. That was news for us—but not just for us. It was for all the people. Good news for the world.

INTERVIEWER: Was that all the angel said? Did he say anything else?

SHEPHERD: Yes! He told us where we would find the baby.

That was the puzzling part. He said, 'This will be a sign to you; you will find a baby wrapped in swaddling clothes and lying in a manger.'

INTERVIEWER: I suppose you all rushed off to see this baby?

SHEPHERD: Well, not right away, because suddenly—while we were trying to take it all in—the heavens exploded with praise. That's the only way I can describe it. An *explosion* of praise!—as if heaven burst open, and angels —hundreds!—*thousands!*—appeared, singing and praising God. I tell you, the world hasn't heard such music since the creation. 'Glory to God in the highest,' they sang. 'And on earth, peace to men on whom his favour rests.'

INTERVIEWER: So, there you were, in the fields with your sheep—and suddenly this remarkable thing happened. An angel spoke to you, a choir of angels sang. What happened then?

SHEPHERD: The angels returned to heaven. It was dark. We felt a sense of loss—going from the lights of heaven into the darkness. But we went to Bethlehem to see what the Lord had told us about.

INTERVIEWER: So you went to see if it was true?

SHEPHERD: No! We didn't go to see if it was true. We *knew* it was true. The Lord—through his angels—had told us. We went and saw the baby, just as the angel had said —wrapped in strips of cloth, lying in a manger. It was strange. The Promised One of God—and he came to be born in a stable and laid in a manger. Do you know what I think? I think we have a God who loves to surprise us.

Easter

5 INTERVIEW—Abraham (*Genesis 22*)

INTERVIEWER: The Easter story was foreshadowed in the Old Testament. The Lord gave many promises and pictures to teach his people how he would bring them to himself. Abraham was one to whom many promises and pictures were given.

Abraham, we have heard that you went to offer a sacrifice with Isaac, your son. Would you like to tell us about it?

ABRAHAM: Yes, of course

INTERVIEWER: Why did you go to make this sacrifice?

ABRAHAM: I went in obedience to God.

INTERVIEWER: What did he tell you to do?

ABRAHAM: God told me, 'Take your son, your only son Isaac, whom you love, and go to the region of Moriah. Sacrifice him there as a burnt offering.'

INTERVIEWER: God ordered you to sacrifice *your son!*

ABRAHAM: When God commands should we not obey?

INTERVIEWER: But Isaac—*your only son!* Were not all God's promises for the future to be fulfilled through Isaac? Surely you must have been horrified?

ABRAHAM: Horrified? No—but I was bewildered. I did not understand. But I knew that God only commands what is good.

INTERVIEWER: So you went to the region of Moriah?

ABRAHAM: Yes. I obeyed God and went out in faith trusting him.

INTERVIEWER: But you were going to offer Isaac as a sacrifice! You were going to kill your own child!

ABRAHAM: I went out not knowing what would happen. It was a journey of faith. When we came to the mountain I told my servants to wait while Isaac and I went up the mountain to worship God. I told them to wait until we came back.

INTERVIEWER: Wait—you said 'till *we* came back.' If you were going to sacrifice Isaac he wouldn't be coming back.

ABRAHAM: As I said, I went out in faith. Faith does not see the future clearly, but can walk into it unafraid. God can be trusted, as I have known these many years

INTERVIEWER: But how could you sacrifice Isaac—and also think that he would come back with you?

ABRAHAM: I was obeying God. So whatever happened would be for the best. The best for myself and the best for Isaac—and all for God's glory.

INTERVIEWER: Did Isaac know you were going to offer him as a sacrifice?

ABRAHAM: No! As we went up the mountain he asked: 'Father, we have the fire and the wood with us, but where is the lamb for the burnt offering?'

INTERVIEWER: How did you answer that?

ABRAHAM: I simply said, 'My son, God himself will provide a lamb.'

INTERVIEWER: So you thought that God would provide a lamb on a barren mountain top?

ABRAHAM: I believed, and trusted, God. And who am I, that I should tell God what to do?

INTERVIEWER: So you went ahead and prepared to sacrifice your only son?

ABRAHAM: I built the altar and bound Isaac ...

INTERVIEWER: But, it seems so inhuman—to be prepared to kill your only son!

ABRAHAM: I was obeying God.

INTERVIEWER: But even so—preparing to kill ...

ABRAHAM: Can the creature say to the Creator what should —or should not—be done?

INTERVIEWER: Even so—to calmly prepare to kill your only son ...

ABRAHAM: Calm!? *I was not calm.* I'm a man. I knew love

and tears for my beloved Isaac. But I knew the God who reigns on high must be obeyed. My eyes were dimmed with tears as I lifted the knife to slay my son, and my hand was shaking. Then came the voice. An angel of the Lord spoke. The very angels of heaven were watching over me and Isaac.

INTERVIEWER: What did the angel say?

ABRAHAM: 'Abraham, Abraham,' said the voice. 'Do not harm the boy. Do not do anything to the lad. Now we know you love God and would not withhold your only son.'

INTERVIEWER: So what happened then?

ABRAHAM: I looked up. I heard the voice, but saw no one. Then I saw a ram caught in a thicket. My words to Isaac were truer than I had thought. God himself had provided a lamb. Is that not a great lesson for us all? It is God himself who provides a lamb.

INTERVIEWER: John saw Jesus coming towards him and said: 'Behold, the Lamb of God, who takes away the sin of the world'—for God so loved the world that he gave his one and only Son, that whoever believes in him shall not perish but have eternal life.

(The following two scripts, 6-7, are set immediately after the death of Christ and before his resurrection. They have their parallel development after the resurrection in scripts 8-10.)

6 TESTIMONY—Pilate

NARRATOR: Who was responsible for the death of Jesus? Many were involved in his execution. Pilate was the Roman Governor in charge. As Governor he would not be interviewed but made the following statement.

PILATE: I am Pontius Pilate, fifth Procurator Of Judea, Roman Governor of this Jewish rabble. As soldier and politician, I am answerable to Rome alone for my actions. What I have done, I have done. I do not need to explain my behaviour to anyone. But, considering the current controversy of this crucifixion, it may be politically expedient to give my account of the matter. Whatever the rights or wrongs of the case against this Jesus, I was in a difficult position. My responsibility is to keep the Roman peace and uphold Roman justice. That is not easy in this land.

The reports about Jesus at his trial were contradictory and some of the things said seemed to be nonsense. They said he was trying to make himself a King, but he certainly did not look like a King to me. He was only a carpenter with ideas. Just a carpenter gone wrong. The strange thing is that when I asked him if he was a king, he replied: 'My Kingdom is not of this world.'

As soldier and politician, I am not interested in any other world than this one. I realised that this was only another religious squabble. These Jews are always arguing about their religion. So what was I to do with Jesus? Even my wife seemed to be caught up in the religious hysteria —she sent a message to me telling of strange dreams and wanting me to have nothing to do with this man Jesus.

I found out that Jesus was from Galilee and sent him to Herod for trial. This was an astute political move because there have been problems of state between King Herod and me. I know he sends reports about me to Rome. So I was glad to get rid of Jesus by sending him to Herod. That has now got me into his good graces. Of course, Herod probably did not realise that I was merely passing on to him an awkward problem. But he sent the prisoner back to me. He—like the rest of the Jews—wanted Jesus dead, but did not have the authority to pass the death sentence.

Caiaphas, the High Priest, is shrewd and would make an excellent politician. He threatened me by suggesting that if I did not have Jesus executed he would undermine my standing in Rome. Such threats never influence me, but I am a politician and offered a compromise. I ordered Jesus to be whipped. I thought that would satisfy their taste for blood. A Roman whipping is real punishment. We have a whip with tiny bones and nails which rip a man's back bare to the bone.

But that wasn't enough for the Jews. They still howled for his death. Then, as an act of Roman clemency, I offered them a choice of prisoners—Jesus or Barabbas. The choice was a vile and violent murderer or a good man. They chose Barabbas.

It's strange, but during all this time, Jesus remained calm and serene. I could not understand that. In the midst of that crazed mob, he seemed the only sane man.

I knew he had done nothing worthy of death. But I was facing a real problem. I had a choice to make—justice or peace. Justice told me he was innocent. But for the sake of peace I had to let him die. So I handed him over to be crucified. But before that, I publicly stated I could find no fault in Jesus and I washed my hands of the whole affair. His death does not lie at my door.

Now he is dead and I am glad it is all over. We will hear no more of him.

7 INTERVIEW—Mary

NARRATOR: Who killed Jesus? What about the friends of Jesus. What have they to say?

Mary, you were one of the followers of Jesus, weren't you?

MARY: Yes, that is right.

NARRATOR: What are your thoughts, now that he is dead?

MARY: Thoughts!? This is no time for thoughts. It's a time for feelings, a time for tears.

NARRATOR: Well, what are your feelings?

MARY: Guilt, remorse, sorrow, self-pity, condemnation. It's hard to find words when there is nothing but emptiness that can only be expressed in tears.

NARRATOR: Yes, but ...

MARY: You see, we ran away and left him. We are all guilty. Judas, whom we trusted, betrayed him. Thomas, who once dared us all to go and die with him, ran away. Even Peter, who had vowed to die with him, three times publicly denied even knowing him.

NARRATOR: But surely it is understandable ...

MARY: Understandable? That we deserted the truest friend we ever had? Understandable that none of us shouted for Jesus instead of Barabbas? No. It was naked fear and cowardice. We helped to drive the nails into his hands and feet.

NARRATOR: But *you* were not responsible for his crucifixion!

MARY: Our unbelief must have been more painful to him than the Roman nails.

NARRATOR: Is it true you were at the foot of the cross when he died?

MARY: It was his mother who wanted to go. She insisted on going. We couldn't let her go alone. So John and some of the women went with her. We went in fear and trembling. I was right, we should not have gone—and yet— have you ever seen a man crucified? Pray God that you never do. It must be the most cruel expression of man's brutality.

NARRATOR: Why do you think it happened?

MARY: We all wanted rid of him, I suppose. Yes—maybe it was as simple as that. Caiaphas, Pilate, the crowd, even his disciples and friends. We all wanted rid of him. When you love the dark, it is not comfortable living with the light.

NARRATOR: Wait, I'm not sure if I follow you ...

MARY: No, I can't follow it all myself. We thought he would be the one to redeem Israel. We thought he was the Promised One of God, the Christ. Now he is dead. No, I don't understand.

NARRATOR: What don't you understand?

MARY: Anything ... everything ...

NARRATOR: But hadn't you followed him for some time? How long have you known him?

MARY: I was there when he came to John the Baptist. It's three years ago now. I keep wondering if that is the key —but I can't think clearly. He is dead and now there is no thought.

NARRATOR: You think John the Baptist is the key?

MARY: The Lamb of God who takes away the sin of the world.

NARRATOR: What does that mean? What are you saying?

MARY: I don't know ... oh, I don't know.

NARRATOR: Then why did you say it?

MARY: I didn't say it. It was John the Baptist. 'Look,' he said, and pointed to Jesus, 'The Lamb of God who takes away the sin of the world.' That seems a long time ago now. A lamb must die to become a sacrifice. But can a man be a lamb? He is dead and what can we do? Where can we go? It has all ended on a cross and there is only guilt and sorrow.

NARRATOR: Mary, tell me—who do you think was really responsible for Jesus' death?

MARY: All of us. We are all guilty. Our rebellion against God, our hatred of the good, our love of ourselves, all nailed him to that cross. *We* killed him—friend and foe alike. But is he, the Lamb, dying for us? I don't know. How can we know? It has all ended, but I can't believe it really is the end. But it must be, mustn't it?

Oh, please, leave me alone—leave me to mourn by myself and weep my own tears and dream my own dreams. Reality is so painful. Where is God? Is death the ultimate reality? ... Oh, where is God?

8 POST-RESURRECTION INTERVIEW— Caiaphas

INTERVIEWER: Immediately after the death of Jesus, the general opinion was that we had heard the last of him. But now there are stories that Jesus has risen from the dead.

Caiaphas—you are the High Priest of the people of Israel. You were largely responsible for the death of Jesus. What do you think of this latest development?

CAIAPHAS: What development?

INTERVIEWER: Surely you have heard—Jesus is reported to have risen from the dead.

CAIAPHAS: That's all a fabrication, a tissue of lies. I have no comment to make.

INTERVIEWER: But there are many reports ...

CAIAPHAS: *Reports!?* Reports from whom? Fishermen? Illiterate peasants? Hysterical women? Who is going to listen to people like that? They don't know what they are talking about.

INTERVIEWER: But what about the tomb?

CAIAPHAS: What about it?

INTERVIEWER: It's empty.

CAIAPHAS: So *they* say ... peasants, fishermen.

INTERVIEWER: But you seemed to be troubled by the tomb after he was buried.

CAIAPHAS: What do you mean?

INTERVIEWER: You ordered soldiers to guard the tomb.

CAIAPHAS: That was purely a precautionary measure. I remembered that he had claimed he would rise from the dead.

INTERVIEWER: So you thought that a resurrection might happen?

CAIAPHAS: Of course not. I am the High Priest and should be treated with respect—so do not put words into my mouth.

INTERVIEWER: But why the soldiers … ?

CAIAPHAS: To stop his misguided disciples stealing the body. I regret it didn't work. They have stolen the body.

INTERVIEWER: But what about the soldiers?

CAIAPHAS: They fell asleep.

INTERVIEWER: It's hard to believe that Roman soldiers were asleep on duty.

CAIAPHAS: I tell you, they were asleep.

INTERVIEWER: There are reports that say you bribed the soldiers to admit they fell asleep.

CAIAPHAS: Are you doubting my word as High Priest? I tell you the disciples stole the body.

INTERVIEWER: Why?

CAIAPHAS: What do you mean, *why*?

INTERVIEWER: What did the disciples have to gain by stealing the body of Jesus and then claiming that he had risen from the dead?

CAIAPHAS: Do you expect me to understand the thinking of such illiterate, ignorant and worthless men? I tell you they stole the body.

INTERVIEWER: High Priest, what are you going to do now?

CAIAPHAS: Ignore the whole thing. I have my religious duties to perform. I have more important things to do than run about after that Jesus of Nazareth.

INTERVIEWER: But supposing it is true? Supposing he really has risen from the dead?

CAIAPHAS: *Risen?* Risen from the dead? No! I refuse to believe it. He is dead. I, the High Priest of Israel, have spoken. Jesus is dead. Ignore him. I have no more to say!

9 POST-RESURRECTION INTERVIEW—
Pilate

INTERVIEWER: What was the reaction of Pilate, the Roman Governor who ordered the execution of Jesus, to the story of the empty tomb?

Your Excellency, Pontius Pilate, would you care to make a statement about the recent events in Jerusalem?

PILATE: Which recent events?

INTERVIEWER: About Jesus of Nazareth, and the reports that he has risen from the dead.

PILATE: Oh, yes—I have heard some garbled reports about that.

INTERVIEWER: What is your reaction to the reports, your Excellency?

PILATE: I washed my hands of that man Jesus after the trial. It has nothing to do with me now.

INTERVIEWER: But he was crucified. You signed the authorisation for his execution.

PILATE: Yes, but I publicly proclaimed that he was innocent. He had done nothing worthy of death. His blood is on their hands, not mine.

INTERVIEWER: But he was crucified—and now they say he is risen from the dead.

PILATE: The people should have let him go. But they howled for his blood. They chose Barabbas.

INTERVIEWER: Your Excellency, do you think it is possible that Jesus has risen from the dead?

PILATE: Of course it isn't possible. When my men kill a man that's the end—he doesn't rise from the dead.

INTERVIEWER: Are you sure he was really dead?

PILATE: When my soldiers crucify someone they don't make mistakes. They have a lot of experience in that sort of thing. Anyway, I remember being surprised at how quickly he had died—he couldn't have been a very strong man. He was dead all right. The Centurion reported that he plunged a spear into his side to make sure. Joseph buried him. You don't bury the living.

INTERVIEWER: But now the tomb is empty.

PILATE: Caiaphas had a guard on the tomb. Go and ask him about it.

INTERVIEWER: We have, your Excellency. He said the guards fell asleep and the disciples of Jesus stole the body.

PILATE: He said that, did he? Yes—*he would*. You can tell Caiaphas that Roman soldiers do not sleep on duty. It's more than their life's worth.

INTERVIEWER: But Excellency, have you *any* theory about what might have happened?

PILATE: Not really—it's probably something to do with their religion. When I saw Caiaphas and that man I knew there would be trouble. I should have listened to my wife. She told me to have nothing to do with that man, Jesus.

INTERVIEWER: But what has a man rising from the dead got to do with religion? I mean, he either rose from the dead or he didn't.

(Pause—Pilate does not answer)

I mean, your Excellency, let me put it this way—do you believe he rose from the dead?

PILATE: I don't know. Well, no, of course he didn't. How

could he? He was dead and the dead don't rise. Unless he was a god. I remember in the courtroom, when I look-ed at him I suddenly thought—no, now wait a minute, I washed my hands of him at the trial. I can only wash my hands again. Enough. Go away. I have nothing further to say—(*he turns away in thought*)—unless he really was a god ....

10 POST-RESURRECTION INTERVIEW— Mary

INTERVIEWER: It is reported that Jesus has risen—Mary, I believe you are claiming to have seen Jesus?

MARY: (*Excitedly*) It's not just a claim—it's true. I saw him. I spoke to him. I touched him. He spoke to me. He is risen. He is alive. I have seen him and ...

INTERVIEWER: Yes, alright, but I wonder if we could go through the events of that Sunday morning.

MARY: It is the same Jesus. I saw him and he is really alive.

INTERVIEWER: Yes, but could you tell us about that Sunday morning when you first saw him. What happened?

MARY: (*Pause*) That Sunday morning. Yes, yes, I'll never forget it. Because they had to bury him in a hurry that Fri-day evening, we had no time to anoint his body. Some of us arranged to go to the tomb early on Sunday morning to do so. It was the least we could do. So we went to the tomb, still very sad, and …

INTERVIEWER: (*Interrupts*) Are you sure you went to the right tomb?

MARY: Have you ever buried someone you loved? Do you then forget where they are buried? Of course we went to the right tomb. How could we forget it?

INTERVIEWER: What did you talk about on the way?

MARY: We didn't talk. You don't talk in the face of death, do you? What is there to say? (*Pauses*) No, wait a minute, we did talk. We thought of the huge stone in front of the tomb and wondered if we could roll it away. It was something we hadn't considered. But when we got there the stone was rolled away.

INTERVIEWER: That must have been a surprise for you. What did you think?

MARY: We didn't know what to think. Had someone stolen the body? It was the sort of cruel thing those who hated him would do.

INTERVIEWER: What did you do?

MARY: We went forward and saw the tomb was empty. I ran to tell Peter and John. I thought maybe they could explain or help. I left the other women and ran to get them.

INTERVIEWER: What did Peter and John say? How did they react? Did they come to the tomb with you?

MARY: Yes. The other women had left when we got there. John ran on ahead and I was with Peter. John just stood outside the tomb, but Peter went right inside. That was just like him. Then we all went in. The tomb was empty. The grave clothes were lying in the place where we left his body and the head square was folded separately. It was all so tidy. I just stood there and wept. John didn't say anything but looked as if he knew something. Then he and Peter went back to see the other disciples.

INTERVIEWER: Did you go with them?

MARY: No, although they wanted me to. But I wanted to be alone. I just stood outside the tomb crying. It was then it happened. It happened!

INTERVIEWER: What happened?

MARY: Suddenly I became aware of somebody there. A man. I thought it was the gardener. I thought he might know where the body of Jesus had been taken, so I asked him.

INTERVIEWER: What did he say?

MARY: 'Mary,' he said. Just my name: 'Mary.' It was him. Jesus. *Alive!*

INTERVIEWER: With all your grief and tears, could you not have been mistaken. Are you sure it was Jesus?

MARY: If someone who loves you says your name in love, it's different from the way anyone else says your name. But it was more than his voice. It was his face, his body— it was him, my Jesus, alive. I wanted to embrace him, to hold him. But he told me not to hold him. He told me to go and tell the other disciples. He was alive. He was going to his Father and my Father, to his God and my God. That's what he said. Imagine! His God was my God—his Father was my Father. Isn't it exciting? He is alive! Death could not hold him. It is the greatest event that has ever happened in the history of all creation. Jesus is alive. The same Jesus who knows me by name.

No, I don't claim he is risen from the dead. *I know.* I have met him. Jesus is alive for evermore!

Pentecost

11 LETTER—John (*John 14-16*)

Dear *Mark*,

This is a hasty scribbled note. I am troubled, confused and depressed. As you know, the Master is dead and the future is dark. I do not know what will happen now. But my mind keeps going back to the supper we had last night, and some of the things he said. They haunt my mind. Perhaps his words contain hope for the future. But for now all is dark and un-certain.

Last night, the evening of the Passover, Jesus said many things. He taught us a lot about the Holy Spirit, stressing the Spirit is a person. Of course we know a lot about the Spirit from the Scriptures. He was the one who descended on the Prophets, calling them to special tasks and fitting them for the Lord's service.

In speaking of the Spirit, Jesus used the word 'Paraclete'— one who comes alongside to help, like an advocate, a com-forter, a teacher. But in his teaching Jesus seemed to be developing the idea much further than any of us had realised. I must confess I do not know fully all that he meant.

It was hard for us to concentrate on his words. He hinted that he was going away—and it would be for our benefit! We could not see how it could be beneficial for us to be left without him. The very thought of living without the Master was frightening. Now we have to do it.

He seemed to be trying to comfort us by this promise of the Spirit. He told us, as I have said, the Spirit would be our comforter. But much more than that; he would be the one who would lead us into all truth and be our teacher. Further, the Master said the Spirit would testify about him, Jesus. In other words, the Spirit would be the revealer and a proclaimer of Jesus. What can such words mean?

The way Jesus spoke, he seemed to suggest that the Spirit would not just come to us, his followers. He would come to men and women who did not follow the Master—to convict them of sin, and righteousness, and judgement. It is all so strange. My mind is so confused.

I have just remembered, when the Master spoke about the Spirit testifying, he added that we, too, must testify about him. He seemed to imply that, with the Spirit, we should be his witnesses on earth!

What does it all mean? I do not know. But I felt last night— and still feel—that we are missing something.

I must go—word has just come that the body of Jesus is missing from the tomb. Some hysterical women are saying he has risen from the dead. I had better go and comfort them and see what is happening.

John

12 INTERVIEW—Woman at Pentecost

INTERVIEWER: There were strange happenings at that first Pentecost in Jerusalem. Suppose we could interview a woman from the crowd that day, what would she tell us?

You are from Jerusalem and saw the events that took place.

WOMAN: No, I'm actually from Crete. But I believe in God

and had come to Jerusalem for the festival. I was going to the Temple that morning when I saw a crowd gathering. I went over to see—and got the shock of my life.

INTERVIEWER: Why, what happened?

WOMAN: I heard a man preaching in my own language. Not many people here can speak the language of Crete. So it was a delightful surprise.

INTERVIEWER: But not many people would be listening to him, would they?

WOMAN: That was the strange thing. There was a group of these men and everyone was listening to them with intense interest. The man next to me said, 'Imagine! He's speaking Persian.' Another said, 'This one is speaking Egyptian.' And I could hear my own language.

INTERVIEWER: I was told the men who were preaching were drunk.

WOMAN: They weren't drunk! It was only nine o'clock in the morning! In fact Peter knew what people were saying and publicly denied that they were drunk. They were just excited at what had happened to them.

INTERVIEWER: Why were they excited? What had happened to them?

WOMAN: I spoke to one of the disciples later and he told me. They were followers of Jesus, who was raised from the dead by God. He had told them to wait until they received power from the Holy Spirit.

INTERVIEWER: We've heard rumours about this Jesus rising from the dead. But you still haven't told us what actually happened.

WOMAN: The disciples found it hard to explain. There came a sound like a rushing wind, then what seemed like flames of fire hovered over each of them. They found they were filled with a power they had never known. They even found they could speak in different languages. As Peter told the crowd, it was a fulfilment of Jesus' promise.

INTERVIEWER: That's interesting. But what were they saying?

WOMAN: It was a simple message, all about Jesus—Jesus, the man of miracles, wonders and signs—how he was put to death on the cross, but God raised him from death. Peter went on to preach a sermon. He told us how this Jesus was the promised one of God, foretold by the prophets. And how this Jesus, whom we crucified, is both Lord and Christ. Imagine, we had *murdered* the Promised One of God.

INTERVIEWER: If what he said was true, surely Israel has done a terrible thing. What can we do about it now?

WOMAN: Peter told us what to do. I will never forget his closing words. He said: 'Repent and be baptised, every one of you, in the name of the Lord Jesus Christ, so that your sins may be forgiven. And you will receive the gift of the Holy Spirit. The promise is for you and your children, and for all who are far away—for all whom the Lord our God will call.'

INTERVIEWER: Did you repent and become a believer?

WOMAN: Oh yes! Yes! I know Jesus is the Christ, the Son of the living God. I know that in him my sins are forgiven —and I too have received the gift of the Holy Spirit.

13 INTERVIEW—Man from Corinth

INTERVIEWER: There is a great deal of confusion about the gifts of the Spirit. Perhaps there always has been— certainly at Corinth there were problems. Here we have a man from Corinth who will tell us some-thing about their difficulties.

Perhaps you could tell us something about the church at Corinth?

MAN: We had lots of problems. There were divisions in the church—there was no discipline, there was immorality among members, everybody doing as they thought fit. And we got into a tangle about the gifts of the Spirit. In fact we got a rocket of a letter from Paul about the state of our church. You can read it in the New Testament.

INTERVIEWER: What we are really interested in is the gifts of the Spirit. What exactly was the difficulty at Corinth about this?

MAN: We emphasised the spiritual and the spectacular. Tongues were the really spectacular gift. Everyone thought you must be very spiritual to speak in tongues.

INTERVIEWER: Yes, tongues certainly are a dramatic gift.

MAN: But the temptation of those who have this gift is to say proudly, 'Look at me, look at the gift I have.'

INTERVIEWER: Yes, but surely tongues is only one gift among many. I believe Paul tried to illustrate that no one was more important than another. Did he not refer to the example of our bodies—no part of the body is more important than another. To be whole we need more than heart or brain—we need eyes, nose, ears, feet. All are equally important to the working of the whole body.

MAN: Yes, exactly—there are all sorts of gifts. Indeed, in writing to the church at Rome, Paul says the gifts include prophesying, serving, teaching, encouraging, contributing to the needs of others, leadership and governing. In his letter to us Paul wrote about the gift of administration. Now these might not seem very spiritual gifts. But nevertheless they are gifts of the Spirit to the church.

INTERVIEWER: It must be hard, though, for a highly gifted man to remain humble. I can understand someone being rather proud of spiritual gifts.

MAN: Should a man be proud of something he hasn't earned, hasn't made, that is simply given to him? Of course not! Gifts show the greatness and grace of the giver, not the one who receives. More than that, they are given as Paul reminded us 'for the common good.' Gifts are bestowed for the good of others—not ourselves!

INTERVIEWER: Did Paul tell you what was the greatest gift? After all, surely some must be more important than others?

MAN: Are they? Paul asked us if the eye was more important than the ear. But, yes, he did tell us what the most important thing is. Indeed he wrote a long passage—a prose poem, almost a hymn to love. And he inserted it into the middle of his teaching about gifts. *Love* is the greatest thing of all. And even if we have all the gifts, are able to preach like angels, have all knowledge and faith to remove mountains—but have not love, then we are nothing.

Harvest

14 DIALOGUE—Thanksgiving

ONE: Do you know, I had a remarkable thought last night?

TWO: What?

ONE: It takes the whole world to feed us.

TWO: What do you mean?

ONE: Well, for breakfast yesterday I started with grape-fruit—that came from Israel. Then I had cornflakes—the corn probably came from Canada or America. Then tea from India, with sugar from the West Indies. I had toast with butter and marmalade—it was Irish butter, and the marmalade was made from Spanish oranges. Imagine—all these countries for my breakfast!

TWO: I never thought of that. Then you would probably have coffee later on. Coffee from Brazil.

ONE: Yes, then a snack lunch, a bacon sandwich. Bacon from Denmark.

TWO: I had a date sandwich—dates from Tunisia. Amazing when you think about it.

ONE: For dinner we had lamb—from New Zealand. Potatoes from Cyprus. That was followed by a rice pudding—and rice comes from the Far East, India or somewhere like that.

TWO: I like curried lamb—curry comes from India.

ONE: The children drank coca-cola with their meal—that's from America.

TWO: We went out and had a Chinese meal last night. No guessing where that came from! And it was my wife's birthday yesterday—I bought her a box of Swiss chocolates.

ONE: We ended the day with a cup of cocoa. Cocoa-beans come from Nigeria.

TWO: You're right. It takes the whole world to feed us.

ONE: And isn't it wonderful that God gives us such a variety of foods and drinks to enjoy? We should be thankful.

TWO: I am.

15 INTERVIEW—Psalmist (*Psalm 104*)

INTERVIEWER: Harvest is the time to think of the rich bounty of nature—food and drink in abundance. Many poets have written about the beauties and overflowing riches we receive from Mother Earth.

We have here a poet who wrote a poem long ago to celebrate the glories of the riches and wonderful balance of nature. We know his poem as Psalm 104.

I must say how much I appreciate your poem about the wonderful interlocking of all aspects of nature.

POET: Why do you keep talking about 'nature'? I never mention *nature* in the Psalm.

INTERVIEWER: Yes, but, is it not all about nature—hills, rivers, trees, animals, birds and …

POET: It's about *creation*. That's why I begin the poem with the Lord who alone is the maker of all things. If he created all things, why not call the works of his hands 'creation'? What did 'nature' ever make?

INTERVIEWER: Yes, an interesting point, perhaps. But could you tell us how you came to write this poem?

POET: By looking—something anyone can do if they just open their eyes. All things have their place and purpose in creation. Waters flow down the mountains, springs produce water—all so that animals, and humans, can quench their thirst. Trees grow by the side of the streams—giving shelter to man and beast, and branches for birds to nest in. Isn't it all wonderful to behold?

INTERVIEWER: Today, in the twentieth century, we have come to appreciate 'green issues' and can see the ecological balance in nature.

POET: You're back to this 'nature' again! Why not call it creation? It is God's creation you know.

INTERVIEWER: Yes, I …

POET: (*Interrupts*) Then you talk about green issues and ecological balance as if they are something spiritual. It is the Lord alone who is to be praised. It is he who laid the foundations of the earth, makes the wind his servant, and has set the boundaries of seas and lands. It is he who makes grass grow for cattle to eat, plants and fruit as food for our nourishment. The world does not show some vague ecological balance. It shows the wisdom and providential care of God for his creatures.

INTERVIEWER: I see what you mean. But that's the way we talk today. Everybody talks about 'Mother Nature'.

POET: I see all too well. You call creation 'nature' to save you talking about the Creator. You talk about ecology to avoid acknowledging the wisdom of God. Why do you try to leave God out of your thinking all the time?

INTERVIEWER: But it's just the way we speak nowadays. Our age is a scientific age, which perhaps explains our language.

POET: I know. But can scientists create a tree? No doubt they can analyse an acorn, list its chemical and biological components. But can they make an acorn out of nothing? Can they change the rhythms of the seasons—summer and winter, springtime and harvest? The earth, sea and air are full of God's creatures. Can science make any of them? Isn't all praise due to the Lord?

INTERVIEWER: Yes, yes! I can appreciate your arguments. But we are facing real problems today with pollution and diminishing resources. We have got to look to science to help us.

POET: But not the God of creation? Is that what you mean?

INTERVIEWER: Well, it's not as simple as that. Anyway, doesn't the scientist get his gifts from God?

POET: Of course he does. But the problem is not a scientific problem. It's a moral problem. That's why I ended my poem the way I did.

INTERVIEWER: I was coming to that. After your poem of celebration of nature—sorry, celebration of *creation*—you add what seems to be a cruel prayer. You write, 'But may sinners vanish from the earth, And the wicked be no more.' What do you mean?

POET: Isn't that the answer? It's sin that causes pollution. It's greed that leads to diminishing resources. If the world was filled with God's people, loving him and their neighbour, wouldn't that be Eden regained? Wouldn't every harvest then be a true time of celebration and sharing?

Remembrance

16 TESTIMONY—Old Man

I am only an old man now—my hair is grey, my face lined and my back bent. Only an old man. But I've got memories. I remember the wars. I remember how we fought to rid the earth of evil, to make the world a better place. I remember blackouts and rationing—newspapers filled with battles lost and won, ships sunk and planes missing. Countless millions dead—dying on foreign fields and in strange waters.

And yet—there was a dream. After the war things would be different—better. We won. The war—as all wars must do—ended. We won, and now—looking back—I wonder?

Did we lose that for which we fought? Were we simply swept along powerless on the tide of history? Did we try to control events, shape them for a better, finer world? Or did we only swim with the ebbing tide of dying visions?

And you, young with the strength of youth, will you also be swept along? Controlled by self-centred dreams and selfish visions? You have all the things we did not—leisure, money, affluence. Too late for me, perhaps too dangerous for you.

But we had a dream, a burning, shining vision. We would remake the world—a world of peace and harmony, respect and love, truth and righteousness. But it was only a dream.

Now, I confess, I do not like this world. Perhaps my generation failed you. We did not make this world—and yet, we built it. Forget, if you will, our suffering and disappointments. But please, please an old man. Take up our dream, our feeble vision. Make it a shining beacon in a world without hope. And take up hope—not in princes and armies; not in political systems and leaders, but in the God of hope.

Part II
LIFE OF THE CHURCH

Evangelism

Fellowship

The Church

1 INTERVIEW—Man from Ephesus (*Revelation 2*)

INTERVIEWER: Ephesus was a church which received a message from the Lord. A letter taken down by John and recorded in the book of Revelation.

We have here a member of that church to tell us about the letter, what it meant to him—and what it might mean to us today. Now tell me about the letter. I believe it had a lot of complimentary things in it?

MEMBER: Yes, in some ways it came as a surprise to us. I knew we did a lot of good, but never really thought about it.

INTERVIEWER: What exactly were you complimented on?

MEMBER: Firstly it was for our good works. The Lord knew of our good deeds, for we did care for one another and the poor who surrounded us. In this, of course, we were simply following our Lord's example.

INTERVIEWER: But you were also commended for your patience. What did that mean?

MEMBER: We suffered some hardship. At times, as was common throughout the Empire, Christians were persecuted. We were no exception! So we had to stand for our faith in times of suffering. After all, we had a faith worth living by and dying for. So the Lord was pleased that we were steadfast at a time of mocking and in the face of martyrdom.

INTERVIEWER: It seems to me that you had a strong, faithful and pure church.

MEMBER: We did try to make it a pure church by holding to the doctrines given by our Lord and taught by the Apostles. So we did not tolerate wrong-doing. We wanted to separate ourselves from evil men who would lead the faithful into dangerous paths.

INTERVIEWER: It must have been a very encouraging letter to you. In the light of what you have said you must have been a shining example to the church of your day, and indeed to us in our times.

MEMBER: No! It was not like that at all.

INTERVIEWER: What do you mean?

MEMBER: The Lord does not look only at our actions. He looks into the heart.

INTERVIEWER: But surely, considering all that you did and were, your heart must have been in the right place. After all, you did good works, commended by the Lord himself—you were patient and faithful in suffering, you did not tolerate evil, and you spoke out against wickedness. What could be wrong with a church like that?

MEMBER: The Lord put his finger on the very heart of our failure. A failure we had not realised and which was really crippling our work and witness.

INTERVIEWER: Failure? What do you mean by failure?

MEMBER: We had left our first love.

INTERVIEWER: Your first love? What does that mean?

MEMBER: The Lord said, 'I hold this against you: You have forsaken your first love.' It came as a shock to our hearts when we heard these words. We recognised their truth with pain. First love is a total experience. It is a love that dominates all of life and action. And our first love had been the Lord himself. But we had become more concerned with merely doing the right things.

INTERVIEWER: I am still not sure what you mean. After all you were continuing all your good works, patient serving, and standing for the faith.

MEMBER: Yes! But we were just going through the motions. We were doing good works because we *always* did good works. We were patient and we persevered because that is what we were expected to do. It was now the done thing for us to behave like that. But our hearts were not overflowing with love for our Lord and the lost in the world.

INTERVIEWER: I think I see what you mean.

MEMBER: Don't do good because it's the respectable thing to do. Don't preserve the church from evil with cold hearts. The first and great commandment is, 'Love the Lord your God with all your heart, soul, mind and strength.' He must be the first love. A church which leaves its first love is in danger of becoming formal, cold and ultimately, dead!   (*cf Revelation 2:1-7*)

49

2 REPORT—On Pergamum, Thyatira, Sardis

I am not a Christian. I am simply a reporter. I try to be honest in my reporting, but at times it is not easy. Recently my editor asked me to do a survey of some churches. He suggested the churches at Pergamum, Thyatira and Sardis.

PERGAMUM: This is certainly a church in a difficult situation. It has many temples and is the centre of many pagan cults. The worship of the Roman Emperor is dominant, so it has not been easy for these Christians who refuse to worship the Emperor. Instead they worship a Jesus, whom they claim was god in human form. Not only that, but they claim he is Lord and King over all—something that does not go down well with the Emperor. In this situation, it is remarkable that they have survived at all. But they have persevered in their faith and are to be commended in this loyalty.

But surprisingly, they tolerate false doctrines and heretics among their members. This is hard to understand. Here are a people who apparently stand fast in their faith, yet are tolerant of those who would corrupt that faith. This does not make sense.

THYATIRA: This seems to be a good church. There is love, and that love is worked out in practice as they perform many good deeds for one another, and the community. This sort of Christian witness seems to be growing and developing.

However, amazingly, they have little discipline, and they seem to tolerate immorality and adultery. This is something I find very hard to understand. There can be no doubt Christianity has the highest moral standard of all our religions. Yet here is a church which apparently accepts immorality in its midst and does absolutely nothing about it!

SARDIS: This is a different type of church. There are some good people in it. But, in general, the church gives the impression of being alive, while really dead. They go through the motions of being busy, active, living. But it is all a sterile duty.

I must confess, I am attracted to Christianity. Unlike our other religions it seems to be based on historical events. This Jesus, whom they worship, did live in Palestine and was crucified under Pontius Pilate. The evidence that he actually rose from the dead seems to be strong.

What attracts me to Christianity is the Christians themselves. But here is a paradox. When I see what is happening in some of the churches, I begin to wonder. I have looked briefly at Pergamum, Thyatira and Sardis. How can Christians act this way—tolerating false teaching, practising immorality, just going through dull routines?

They have the teachings of their God in a book and yet willingly accept teaching which denies what it says. In being called to follow the One whom they claim was sinless, how can they condone sexual immorality and adultery? In preaching about the One who claimed to come giving life, how can they be a company of dead people going through the motions of religion?

I find it hard to understand.

(cf Revelation 2:12-3:6)

3 TESTIMONY—Modern Laodicea

It is with pride I present the annual report of our church at Laodicea. It has certainly been another successful year in every department of our church's life. We can take great satisfaction from the happy state of affairs in which we find ourselves.

As our Treasurer's Report shows, we are in a very favourable financial position. Offerings were up by a healthy margin. We received more than we asked for and easily met all our commitments. Indeed, we have a healthy surplus which will be invested to give us a good return in the future. Other churches may well envy us—compared to many we are rich. This is a matter for self-congratulation. Of course, financial matters are not the only way to measure the success of a church. But in all other areas of our congregational life we may humbly claim to be successful.

We have long boasted of the fact that we are a broad church. Tolerance is one of our greatest graces. So we are not a cold church, or a hot one. By that I mean, we do not preach the cold doctrines of orthodoxy or get fired up by hot evangelism. We seek the middle way.

This means we are acceptable in the community. Indeed, we are rapidly becoming a social centre for our town. We are willing to become all things to all men, so that they may find us acceptable to them. We do not embarrass people by expecting them to come to prayer meetings or Bible studies, and other religious activities that divide people and must always encourage spiritual pride.

So, long may our church continue to be a real social asset to our community. We serve the people and see ourselves as being concerned with all the political and social needs of the people. To those who say we should hold to a narrow religion, preaching only one way to God, I say, 'Stand outside our door.' We will continue to be successful as we are.

It gives me great pleasure to present this annual report.

(cf Revelation 3:14-22)

Communion

4 INTERVIEW—Moses on the Passover

INTERVIEWER: Moses brought the Jews out of captivity in Egypt, and set God's law before them.

Moses, you are a great leader, a great prophet of God …

MOSES: Don't call me great. Only God is great. When God called me to be the leader of his people I was reluctant to go. Indeed I kept making excuses not to go …

INTERVIEWER: Yes, but what we really want to know is something about the Passover. You instituted the Passover?

MOSES: No! No! I did not institute the Passover. It was God who did that—the God who came to the rescue of his people.

INTERVIEWER: Could you tell us about it?

MOSES: Surely you know the story? The people of God were enslaved in Egypt. But God watches over his people and when the time for deliverance was come, he sent me as his messenger. I had to plead with Pharaoh: 'Let God's people go.'

INTERVIEWER: But Pharaoh refused you? He defied you?

MOSES: No, he defied the Living God.

INTERVIEWER: Then what happened?

MOSES: The Lord sent plagues—one plague after another. The rivers and the pools turned to blood so that even the fish died. But Pharaoh would not listen—or obey God. Then there were plagues of frogs, gnats, plagues on the livestock and plagues of boils on men, plagues of hail, locusts, darkness—but still Pharaoh, puffed up in pride, would not listen to the voice of God. He became hardened and bitter against God. Then came the final plague.

INTERVIEWER: But you haven't mentioned the last plague, what you call the Passover. Tell us about that.

MOSES: Yes, the Passover. God sent the angel of death over the land. One dark night every firstborn son died. The firstborn son of every family in the land—from the palace of Pharaoh to the humblest home of the poorest slave. As the angel of death passed over, death struck.

INTERVIEWER: That seems a cruel judgement on many who must have been innocent.

MOSES: Innocent? Who is innocent before a holy God? But even in judgement God offered a way of escape for those who obeyed him. He provided salvation from the angel of death. Salvation for all who took it. All who believed his Word and acted on it—Jew or Egyptian.

INTERVIEWER: Yes, but what was this way of escape?

MOSES: Each household had to take a lamb—a lamb without spot or blemish. If it was a small household, or poor, they could share with their neighbours. They had to kill this lamb. They were to eat it, every part of it, ready to leave the land of bondage.

INTERVIEWER: You mean they were just to have a meal?

MOSES: No! They had to take the blood of the lamb and put it on the sides and tops of the door frames of their homes.

INTERVIEWER: That seems a bit strange. What was the meaning of that?

MOSES: It meant that when the angel of death saw the sign of innocent blood he passed by. Those who had placed themselves under the blood were safe.

INTERVIEWER: It certainly seems to have been an interesting event.

MOSES: It was a tremendous night! But it was more than an event. It was a picture. A picture of how God delivers his people. So that we will never forget this, the Lord has established the Feast of the Passover as a lasting memorial. A lasting memorial and picture of how God saves. Not through our efforts or merit, but through God's grace and the shedding of the blood of an innocent lamb.

*(cf 1 Corinthians 5:7,
Peter 1:18-19, Colossians 1:19-22)*

5 LETTER—John: The Last Passover

Dear *Mark,*

These are hurriedly scribbled notes which I hope you will keep for me. I want to set them down while the events are still fresh in my mind.

At the moment I do not know what is happening. I have just kept the Passover with the Master. He has gone to pray, and the rest of us are about to follow. I am just noting these things down before we go.

It was a strange Passover. We met in the upper room, as you know. It was strange from the beginning. There were no servants—but Jesus got water and a towel and started to wash our feet. He took the place of the lowest servant! Peter objected—he put his foot in it again! He asserted that Jesus would never wash his feet. But Jesus told him straight—'If I do not wash your feet then you have no part of me.'

The Passover is always a solemn event. Tonight there was a solemnity which seemed to touch all our spirits. I had the strange fear that we were keeping it for the last time, though I do not know how such a thing can be.

What really bewilders me is this. Before the actual Passover meal, the Master took bread, broke it and said: 'This is my body, given for you, do this in remembrance of me.' Then after supper, he took wine and said: 'This cup is the new covenant in my blood; do this in remembrance of me.'

This strange, new ritual seemed important to him, I don't know why. It seemed to be a new Feast—a new sacrament. But what does it mean? Bread, wine, blood! He seemed to tie it all to his death. But that does not make sense, does it?

We were bewildered and upset. He comforted us, saying

that we would mourn, but our grief would turn to joy. I am confused. Something terrible is going to happen. It is the bread and wine that trouble me. He instituted what he called a new covenant—but how can that be? We have to do it in remembrance of him! But how can anyone who ever knew him possibly forget?

John

6 LETTER—Indifferent!

Dear *Robert*,

You wrote to ask me to tell you about communion in our church for some project you are working on. I don't know if I can help much. As you may know I am not really a churchy sort of person. Of course, I am a member, and I do make a point of attending communion at least once a year.

I find communion a strange sort of service and I don't quite know what to make of it. So maybe I'm not the right person to ask questions about it. Truth to tell, I don't think it's as nice as it used to be. I liked it better when all the elders were dressed in tail coats and black ties.

The last time I was at a communion service I was really angry. Just because I hadn't been to the last two or three communions I had lost my communion card. The young elder at the door thought I was a visitor! I was annoyed, I can tell you. I have been a member of that church for thirty years or more and a young upstart of an elder thought I was a mere visitor! I gave him a piece of my mind.

When it is communion, the children are not in church, so

there is no children's story. I miss that—our minister is good with the children, and it's the part of the service I like. I will not say anything about hymns. They were dreary, and to make things worse, the minister picked some I didn't even know. I think it's always nice to have a good sing-song, but you can't if they're all dreary hymns about Jesus dying on a cross. I think church should be the place where we get cheered up a bit.

I didn't really pay much attention to the sermon—I have had rather a lot on my mind recently. Jim has been promoted and we are wondering about moving to a bigger house. We've been looking at a few.

Then came the 'distribution of the elements' as they call it (though I'm not sure what that means). Do you know what happened? The elder missed my pew with the bread! I was not at the end of the pew or I would have given him a piece of my mind! However, he came back. I found the bread dry. And I don't know what kind of wine they use, but it was very watery. Anyway, I went away thankful that's it all over for a while.

I hope this will help you.

Andrew

7 LETTER—Inspiring!

Dear *John,*

You wrote asking about our communion service for some project you are working on. I love communion, though I must confess I find it crowded with members who are strangers to me. I find this rather sad. But it is a fact that attendance is usually much greater at our communion service.

It is an inspiring service. I like to think, on going to church that morning, that I am happily doing what the Lord commanded his followers to do—to remember him. I may not be perfect, but this is something I can do with a faithful, humble heart. I can remember him the way he asked me to.

I find the service sad, yet strangely uplifting. Jesus Christ died for me. What an astonishing truth!

As I take the bread and wine, two thoughts seem to dominate my mind. First, I am following a tradition that has continued down through the centuries in every culture and continent. The unworthy disciples of the Galilean have gathered to remember and testify to his death and coming again. I find that a comforting thought, linking me to all the saints who ever lived. I know we can follow different traditions and patterns. But at the heart of all communions are the bread and wine—the simple things he ordained in that Upper Room long ago.

But second, the other thought, which should be the dominant one, is that the bread represents his body, given for me; and the wine, representing his blood, shed for me. The words of Paul always ring in my ears as I take those simple things— bread and wine—'The Son of God who loved me and gave himself for me.'

What a glorious and humbling truth. In spite of my ill-health, material poverty, and daily struggle, I feel uplifted to the very throne of God at each communion service.

Perhaps this will not help you much. I know I have told you more about my own feelings than about the actual service. But surely the mechanics do not matter when the heart is touched with the wondrous love of our Lord Jesus.

Jim

59

c

Baptism

8 DIALOGUE—Bible *versus* Folklore!

MOTHER ONE: Are you getting your baby done soon?

MOTHER TWO: Done? What do you mean, *done*—do you mean inoculated?

MOTHER ONE: No—in church I mean. Christened.

MOTHER TWO: Oh you mean *baptised*. Certainly. I see Jean as a wonderful gift from God.

MOTHER ONE: Well, that's not quite the way I'd say it, but I want Mary done. And it will need to be soon. Granny says the baby's not right with God until she's properly done in church.

MOTHER TWO: I'm a church member and I certainly want Jean to belong to the family of the church.

MOTHER ONE: I don't go to church very often, but what's that got to do with it? I'll make sure I send her to Sunday School when she's old enough. Oh, and that's another thing. Did you know they'll not take her into Sunday School if she's not been properly done in church?

MOTHER TWO: Who told you that? That's nonsense!

MOTHER ONE: Well, I've been told they have to be done if you want to send them to Sunday School.

MOTHER TWO: That's not true! Anyway I am looking forward to the baptismal service. Apart from anything else it will be my first opportunity for a long while to publicly reaffirm my faith in God as my Father, and Jesus as my Saviour and Lord.

MOTHER ONE: Yes, well, I suppose you're right. I'm not particularly religious. But I'm looking forward to the ceremony. We'll have a party afterwards, a nice family get-together. My husband is already saving up to get the drinks in. The last time it was a real party—my wee boy was done in the morning and the party didn't finish until the small hours. Nothing beats a good party, does it?

MOTHER TWO: Hmm, I suppose we will have a small family gathering. The Grandparents will certainly be there. But I look upon it as a solemn occasion, almost sacred.

MOTHER ONE: You keep bringing religion into it! I just want Mary done.

MOTHER TWO: Yes, but it is religious! What about the vows you and your husband will be taking? Don't they mean anything? It's a serious business trying to bring up a child in the ways of God, teaching the faith and setting an example.

MOTHER ONE: Oh I'm sure the vows don't mean that much. It's just part of the rigmaroll of the church. All I want is to get Mary done so that she'll have the right start with God.

The Bible

9 INTERVIEW—Baruch (*Jeremiah 36*)

INTERVIEWER: Down the centuries many have tried to destroy the Word of God. In Jeremiah, chapter 36, there is an account of such an attempt. Baruch, the servant of Jeremiah, was involved. Suppose we could ask him to tell us what happened?

You are Baruch, a servant of Jeremiah, his secretary really. We would like to know something about this strange story of how King Jehoiakim treated the Word of God; but first, could you tell us something about Jeremiah?

BARUCH: Oh, he was a Prophet. A Prophet of the living God. He was called by God to speak a word the people did not want to hear. So it was hard for him. He knew much agonised prayer, tears and suffering. But God spoke to him, and through him.

INTERVIEWER: Tell us about this particular incident which I believe started in the Temple.

BARUCH: It really started in Jeremiah's home when God gave him a message for the people. He dictated the words to me and I wrote them down on a scroll. They were words of judgement. Jeremiah was under house-arrest at that time and could not go out, so he asked me to go to the Temple and read out the words the Lord had given.

INTERVIEWER: Did you do that?

BARUCH: Yes!

INTERVIEWER: What was the reaction?

BARUCH: Oh, the usual reaction—total rejection. Men do not want to hear of God's standards, or God's holiness, or God's judgement. Instead of repenting of their sins, humbling themselves before God and trusting him, they mocked and became angry.

INTERVIEWER: I believe the King became involved?

BARUCH: Yes, he had heard about the scroll and wanted to see it for himself.

INTERVIEWER: That surely must have spelled danger for you?

BARUCH: Danger for Jeremiah, not me. I was only a servant. But a friendly court official advised me to get Jeremiah into hiding. I did this before I took the scroll to the King.

INTERVIEWER: What happened then?

BARUCH: The King ordered that the scroll should be read to him. As the reader finished each page, the King took it, and—guess what—he deliberately cut it into strips and threw them into the fire. Can you imagine that? Tearing up God's Word and burning it like worthless rubbish. Some of his advisers were troubled and urged him not to treat the message with contempt. But he burned it all, every page of the scroll, every word of that message from God.

INTERVIEWER: So that word from God was utterly destroyed?

BARUCH: No! No man, no matter how high and great, can ever destroy the Word of God.

INTERVIEWER: But you said it was torn into strips and burned. Did you have a copy?

BARUCH: No. But when Jeremiah heard that the King had burned the message he told me to take another scroll. He dictated the same words over again. So I wrote down all the words which were on the scroll the King had burned. But this time there was more—there was a judgement on the King. No one, King or commoner, can destroy God's Word. It is forever sure. His Word will never pass away.

10 DIALOGUE—Read, or not Read!

ONE: Do you know, I've just rediscovered the Bible. I've just started reading it regularly—and it's great! I find it really exciting.

TWO: The Bible exciting? You won't catch me reading it

ONE: Why not?

TWO: Well, it's such an old-fashioned book. Who would want to read it today?

ONE: But that's the amazing thing! It's not old fashioned at all. I'm continually surprised how relevant it is. Today I was reading First Thessalonians, and the last chapter is full of good sensible advice—all about respecting one another, living in peace together, encouraging and being patient with one another, always being thankful, and ...

TWO: But it's so hard to understand. I mean, it's such old-fashioned language.

ONE: But there are new translations that make it easier to understand.

TWO: I don't like those new translations. They don't sound like the Bible!

ONE: But even our old Bible was once a new translation. Language changes over the years, you know. You should try reading a new translation.

TWO: Yes, well, anyway the Bible is full of unbelievable things.

ONE: Such as?

TWO: Well, surely science has disproved the Bible?

ONE: Oh, you read science books do you?

TWO: No, I don't read science books. But I've heard about science ...

ONE: But many scientists read the Bible. What's more, they *believe* the Bible.

TWO: Yes, but all these miracles in the Bible—how on earth can we believe them?

ONE: Do you believe in God?

TWO: Yes, of course I do.

ONE: So you think God can't perform miracles?

TWO: No, I wouldn't say that.

ONE: You admit then, that God *can* perform miracles?

TWO: I suppose so. I suppose he can do anything.

ONE: Except miracles—according to you. Anyway, the Bible's not just a book about miracles. It's history, biography, poetry, letters. It tells us that God made and loves the world. It tells us God's laws and commandments which are for our good. It tells us that we have sinned, and how God sent his Son into the world to die for us. The Bible tells how God raised him from the dead. It tells how he will come back to write 'The End' over the story of history and make a new heaven and a new earth.

TWO: That's all too complicated for me. I don't read the Bible—I just try to live as a Christian—surely that's the important thing?

ONE: But what standard do you use in trying to live as a Christian?

TWO: What do you mean?

ONE: Isn't the Bible our guide for living?

TWO: Yes, no—well, I just try to follow Jesus.

66

Prayers

11 LETTER—Rhoda (*Acts 12*)

Dear *Dorcas,*

The most amazing thing has happened. It was truly remarkable, in fact miraculous. I must tell you about it. It really
shows the power of prayer. But, to be honest, it also shows
how we sin by not trusting the Lord.

Jesus truly is Lord and God. Remember how, when he
lived among us, he was a man of miracles. He is still the
same today. I have seen his power. What a wonderful Saviour
we have in the Lord Jesus!

But I must tell you what happened. I don't know if you
heard, but King Herod has turned against us, the followers
of the Lord. He has put many in prison, and among them
was Peter. We feared for Peter's life. Herod knows that he is
one of our leaders, and would not hesitate to put Peter to
death.

We did the only thing we could do. We prayed. We all
gathered in the house of Mary, Mark's mother. That is the
house where I am a servant. We all prayed, pouring out our
fears and hopes to the Lord for our beloved Peter. We asked
the Lord to spare him, to soften Herod's heart so that we
might have Peter among us again. We have had many prayer
meetings here but this one was the most moving I have ever
attended. We pleaded with tears for the Lord to act and
rescue Peter from the hands of the King.

Suddenly there was a heavy knock at the door. As the
servant of the house it was my duty to answer. I went with
fear and trembling, afraid it was Herod's soldiers come to

arrest us. I was fearful I would deny my Lord if I had to suffer for him.

Rather than open the door I shouted, and asked who was there. A voice answered, 'It's me, Peter!' It was Peter's voice. I would have recognised it anywhere.

Then, do you know what I did! I forgot to open the door, and dashed back into the room. Interrupting the prayers I shouted, 'It's Peter—Peter is free, and at the door!' I was so excited, so full of joy—I was screaming the news. But did they believe me? They thought I was hysterical, out of my mind! So there was I, trying to convince them, and poor Peter hammering at the door to get in.

Somebody went and opened the door and, sure enough, it was Peter. He got some welcome, I can tell you. Peter told us what had happened. He had been in chains, two guards at his cell door, when the dungeon had flooded with light and an angel appeared. The angel told Peter to get dressed, and led him out of the prison, all the doors miraculously opening.

It was a real miracle. But how shamefully we acted. We were praying for Peter's release and when God answered our prayers we did not believe it! But how good is our Lord Jesus. He told us to pray and believe—we prayed and doubted! How little faith we have!

Yours in his glorious name,

Rhoda

12 DIALOGUE—Prayer Meeting

ONE: What do you think of this idea of having a prayer meeting?

TWO: I think it's a good idea. It's something we need.

ONE: Is that what you think?

TWO: Why, don't you want a prayer meeting?

ONE: Not me! I've no time for all these new-fangled ideas they keep bringing into the church.

TWO: But it's nothing new! There have been prayer meetings for thousands of years. We even read of them in the book of Acts. The early church had meetings where they all met for prayer.

ONE: That's what I mean—it's an old-fashioned idea.

TWO: Make up your mind. It's either new or old-fashioned —it can't be both.

ONE: Anyway, I think the church is doing fine without prayer meetings.

TWO: Church doing fine? Have you looked at our numbers? We've lost about half our membership in the last twenty years.

ONE: The church doors are open every Sunday, I always say. They can come if they want.

TWO: But they *don't* come!

ONE: And do you really think they'll come if we have a prayer meeting?

TWO: Well, not necessarily. But we certainly need God's help. We are not doing very well on our own.

ONE: I think prayer meetings are maybe all right for religious folk—but not for the likes of me.

TWO: What do you mean religious folk? You're a member of the church—an elder—you come regularly. Does that not make you religious?

ONE: You know what I mean! I'm not sure a prayer meeting would make any difference.

TWO: It would mean that we come as a family to our Father, asking his help to build up our church. Surely that could only be for the good.

ONE: Maybe. But I don't know if it's for the likes of me. I mean, what good would it do me?

TWO: Well, there's fellowship. We are all equal before the throne of God. We come as a family, genuinely seeking his help, not only for ourselves, but for all those who need him. After all, we are commanded to pray for one another, for those in authority, for all people.

ONE: Maybe the way the Government's acting they could do with somebody praying for them.

TWO: Not only that. We could learn a lot. We would share our own needs for prayer, and our interests as well. Some are interested in foreign missions, child abuse, animal welfare and many other things. It would be good for us to learn from one another so that we can pray intelligently.

ONE: Yes, well, maybe so—but I don't think you'll get me at a prayer meeting.

TWO: Why not?

ONE: For one thing I would be embarrassed. I couldn't stand up and pray out loud like those religious folk do.

TWO: But you don't need to pray out loud. It's not compulsory. God can hear the prayers of our hearts and minds. Anyway I don't know why you keep having digs at the 'religious folk.' I think Jesus was pretty religious, don't you?

ONE: This prayer meeting—it's going to be held on a Thursday night. That doesn't suit me.

TWO: But that's only a suggested night. What night would suit you?

ONE: I don't know. I'm pretty busy you know.

TWO: But we could change the night ...

ONE: Oh, you don't need to change anything for me. My week's pretty full as it is.

TWO: How about a monthly prayer meeting?

ONE: I keep trying to tell you. I don't think prayer meetings are for the likes of me.

TWO: Well, I know they are for the likes of *me*. And God certainly thinks they are for the church.

Worship

13 INTERVIEW—Amos on Worship

INTERVIEWER: Amos, you are one of the prophets of God. A man with a message about social justice. But I would like to ask you about something else—worship. Do you think worship is important, or should we devote our time and energy fighting for justice and a fair society?

AMOS: But you can't separate them. Worship comes first— isn't the first commandment to love the Lord our God with all our heart, soul, mind and body?

INTERVIEWER: Would you argue that it is important to gather together in worship?

AMOS: Important! It's crucial. Wasn't it that which the Lord gave me to declare, 'Seek me and live'? How can we know life unless we turn to the Lord.

INTERVIEWER: But what is the important element in worship?

AMOS: God himself. He must be fundamental, central to all our worship. He is God—the Creator—the Holy One. Our hearts and minds must be filled with him alone. Offering ourselves to him is true worship.

INTERVIEWER: But what about the mechanics of worship? I mean, the place where we meet and the things that we do must be taken into consideration.

AMOS: No, no—it's the heart that is important. The people in my day had hearts far from God. Yet they thought that if they had pilgrimages to Bethel, to Gilgal, to Beersheba —then God would welcome them. But it was not so. God despised their religious feasts, and all their fine singing and music. He would not accept them because their hearts belied their worship.

INTERVIEWER: But surely temples, churches, sacred places of worship are important?

AMOS: A heart open to God, a heart that seeks good and hates evil—that is the source of worship to God, wherever it is.

INTERVIEWER: But what about social justice? You are the great prophet of social justice. Where does that fit into worship?

AMOS: We must come to God and be right with him. We must worship him. Only then can we go out to proclaim the need for justice and righteousness in the land.

INTERVIEWER: But how can we be right with God?

AMOS: What was it David said—'A broken and a contrite heart you will not despise.' We simply throw ourselves on God's mercy. He accepts us. Then our worship becomes true. Our worship then flows from the heart—love towards the God of holiness who loves us. That love then demands action, action in a fallen world where there is sin and injustice and cruelty.

INTERVIEWER: If I understand you correctly, you are

73

saying that true worship leads to action?

AMOS: Of course! If we love God, how can we not love all his creatures? How can we not love all his people? Then the prayer in our heart will become the desire in our lives. To see justice roll like a river and righteousness like a never failing stream.

INTERVIEWER: Are you making worship and service the same thing? Are you saying that we can worship God by doing good actions?

AMOS: How can they be the same thing? We worship God. We lift up our heart and mind to him, praising him with our lips. And being in his presence, even for short hours of worship, should be a life-changing experience. Our eyes have been on eternity—then we can turn, better equipped to face the demands of time. True worship always leads to action.

14 DIALOGUE—
Routine *versus* Enthusiasm!

ONE: That was a good service, wasn't it?

TWO: I suppose so.

ONE: You don't sound very enthusiastic.

TWO: Well, to tell you the truth, I found it a bit dreary. In fact, I suppose I usually find it a bit dreary.

74

ONE: Then why do you come?

TWO: Habit, I suppose. I've always come to church. My wife was keen and I usually went with her. Now that she's gone I just keep up the habit. But sometimes I think I would be as well staying at home on Sunday mornings. Don't you ever find it dreary?

ONE: Oh no! I love going to church. I'm always back at night as well. It's something I look forward to. God always has some surprises for me. I always get something out of it.

TWO: Well, I didn't this morning. I didn't know that first hymn and then that last—it was a new tune, wasn't it? Anyway the singing was pathetic. There was someone singing off key at every hymn.

ONE: Oh, that was probably me! I'm tone deaf, but I just love singing. I love lifting my heart and voice to God for all he has done for me. Maybe I can't keep in tune, or in the right key. But God has some croaky birds as well as nightingales and larks. I'm sure he hears me singing from the heart.

TWO: Well, maybe. I don't think that way. Maybe I'm not really very churchy.

ONE: It's got nothing to do with being churchy. God wants us to gather to worship him. I find it exciting and heart-warming to be with his people singing his praises—in tune or not.

TWO: Mind you, I like the children's address. Where does the minister get them all from. But I don't like the prayers.

ONE: The prayers touch my heart. It must be hard to gather up all the prayers of a congregation and put them into words.

TWO: I find the prayers long and dreary.

ONE: Prayers dreary? I don't find that. Although sometimes I wonder if God ever gets bored with some of the things I tell him.

TWO: Do you mean that you pray away from church?

ONE: Of course—you don't think God only hears us in church, do you?

TWO: I think that's carrying things a bit far. Anyway, it's enough to sit through long-winded prayers in church without making up my own.

ONE: But don't you have anything to thank God for—or that you need to ask him—every day?

TWO: I do go to church, but as I keep telling you, I'm not really a religious sort of person. Those pew Bibles, for instance. Imagine being expected to look up the reading! We didn't have them in the past. Why start now?

ONE: I suppose it is because we have stopped bringing our own Bibles to church. I find it helpful—easier to understand. And sometimes it brings my attention to parts of the Bible I haven't read before. That's why I bring my own Bible. I put a marker in and read it again when I get home. Anyway, what did you think of the sermon this morning?

TWO: Not much! My mind tends to wander. I've got rather a lot on my mind just now.

ONE: That's just the time you should listen. I find it amazing how often when I am troubled about something, I get a word of help which I am sure is straight from God. Not just comfort—often I get a challenge about the sort of life I am living. I don't know what I would do without church.

TWO: That's your opinion. I mean I am happy to go—well, because I *always* go.

ONE: But isn't it wonderful how, in this country, we are free to do what God wants us to do? Join together with others to worship him, sing his praises, ask his blessing, listen to his Word, and go out with his benediction ringing in our ears. What a wonderful privilege.

Evangelism

15 DREAM—On Trial

NARRATOR: It was a dream. It must have been a dream, a dream such as I have never known. I stood in the dock of some court, but all around me was shadowy darkness. I could only assume it was a dock. Then came a voice from the darkness. I could not see the speaker, I was only conscious of the accusing voice.

VOICE: Guilty—or not guilty?

NARRATOR: Guilty of what?

VOICE: You are a member of the church. A man who took vows to serve the Lord and his church. Have you fulfilled those vows?

NARRATOR: I've tried to. I mean, I know I've failed in many ways, but I've tried to serve as well as I could.

VOICE: How about evangelism?

NARRATOR: What do you mean—evangelism?

VOICE: Evangelism, outreach, witness, mission. Are you a member of a growing church which is ever seeking to make new disciples for the Lord?

NARRATOR: Well, we don't really go in for that sort of thing? I mean the church doors are open every Sunday and if anyone wants to come they are welcome.

VOICE: Welcome to come in and sit anywhere?

NARRATOR: Well, some people like their own seats, but that's only human nature.

VOICE: But you don't go out of your way to try to bring people in?

NARRATOR: No, as I say, the door is open for anyone who wants to come in.

VOICE: And did your Master say, 'Let the door be open for all who want to come in'?

NARRATOR: I don't know—I ...

VOICE: Did he not say, 'Go into all the world and preach the gospel'?

NARRATOR: Oh, *that's* what you mean? Well, we have a missionary partner whom we support. He's in Malawi, I think. We send him a present every Christmas. And we support Christian Aid. So I suppose we do our bit for the world.

VOICE: But what about the world around your church doors? What about the clubs and pubs in your parish? What about the broken homes, broken families, broken hearts around the church where you worship? Do you go to them?

NARRATOR: I think the minister does what he can. But he's

pretty busy you know—we have a large congregation.

VOICE: And did your Master say, 'Let all missionaries and ministers go into all the world to preach the gospel'?

NARRATOR: But that's their job.

VOICE: Was the Lord not speaking to all his people?

NARRATOR: But we are all busy doing the Lord's work in other areas. I mean we have financial problems to face in trying to keep up the fabric of the church.

VOICE: And is fabric more important than folk? Is that the kind of God you worship—one who wants lovely huge buildings and has little interest in people?

NARRATOR: No, but we need the building. I mean, if the church building fell down there would be no place for us to meet.

VOICE: Perhaps then, you would need to go out into the world.

NARRATOR: Are you suggesting that we should do without our church buildings?

VOICE: I simply ask questions. I do not give answers. You stand accused of disobeying your Lord by not taking his good news into all the world.

NARRATOR: But some of us don't find that our cup of tea. I mean we are not good at that sort of thing.

VOICE: As a child you were not very good at reading, writing, counting. You had to learn how to do these things. Should you not seek to learn how to be a better witness for your Lord?

NARRATOR: But I'm not good at talking and ... I mean I'm not an evangelist.

VOICE: You can pray, can't you? Do you pray for the people and homes around your church? Pray for your friends and neighbours who do not know the Lord? You can live as a Christian—love as a Christian—speak as a Christian.

VOICE: I don't know why you should accuse me of not ...

NARRATOR: I do not accuse you of anything. It is the Lord alone who is Judge. It was he who said, 'Go into all the world and preach the gospel.'

16 DIALOGUE—Church Growth

ONE: Do you ever get depressed about the church?

TWO: What do you mean?

ONE: We seem to belong to a shrinking church, a church that is losing members year by year, and showing little, if any, signs of growth.

TWO: But the church is growing!

ONE: Is your church growing? Increased membership, increased attendance?

TWO: Well, no, not actually *my* church. The church worldwide. It seems to be growing rapidly in Africa, South America, the Far East. Look at Korea—it's booming in these areas. Then in Russia and Eastern Europe—despite years of state dominated atheism, the church grew and continues to grow.

ONE: Yes, that may be true. But what about Europe, our own country in particular—the church is shrinking.

TWO: I agree. We have problems.

ONE: What do you think the answer is?

TWO: Before we can give the answer, maybe we've got to identify the problem.

ONE: What do you think is wrong? I mean, why are we declining? Why do people not come to church?

TWO: I suppose it's the kind of society we live in. It's a materialistic society, people are encouraged to think that only this world matters. It is a world without the spiritual.

ONE: So, it's just the spirit of the age that is against us?

TWO: No! We must all share the blame. Sometimes, perhaps in my more cynical moments, I look at my church and wonder why anyone comes at all.

ONE: I sometimes think that maybe we are too concerned

about the church—as a building or institution—rather than the Lord of the church.

TWO: Yes! We have the problem of old buildings. Huge churches—lovely old buildings—but they are crumbling and falling apart. So we face a financial burden trying to keep a roof over our head.

ONE: The result is the minister ends up as a fund-raiser. We are all caught in the money-raising trap. When you think of the time and effort used in getting our finances right, you wonder what we could do if we devoted all that effort and time to strengthening the church—not as a building, but as a congregation.

TWO: We certainly need to build bigger congregations. We talk a lot about outreach, but I'm not sure we ever actually do anything about it.

ONE: As a last resort we set up a committee!

TWO: Yes, but surely we need to mobilise the congregation —make every member a witness. A team effort to build up the church.

ONE: That's true, but sadly so many of our churches seem to have—or to look upon—their minister as a one-man band.

TWO: And we have elders and leaders in the church who seem to leave nearly everything to the minister.

ONE: Also, too many members simply don't come to church.

TWO: It is depressing, isn't it?

ONE: Too many quite simply don't see *any problem* at all.

17 TESTIMONY—Vision of Tomorrow

I dreamt I lived in a Christian land, a land where God's name was revered, where his Son was worshipped, and where his Spirit guided every heart. It was a land where his Word was read and obeyed, a land where God's commandments were joyously kept.

It was a society that loved and worshipped God and there were no idols. God's name was honoured and never used as an idle oath or a bitter curse. His day was kept holy and millions gathered to sing his praises and hear his Word. Parents were respected and each family reflected heaven's glory. There was no murder, and marriage vows were kept so that broken homes and broken families were unknown. There was no stealing and no lying, for the people respected each other and loved the truth at all times. Then there was no coveting, for all had learned the joy of contentment.

It was a good land—a happy society—a healthy culture. It was a land where there was no loneliness because the people loved, and had time, for one another. The young loved the old, and the old enjoyed the company of the young. The curse of drugs and drunkenness had vanished from the land and life was lived to the full, everyone enjoying the good things of God.

Crime had disappeared. Little children played safely on the streets, and women could walk unafraid in the dark. Newspapers found good news to cheer the readers. Television found it could make righteousness exciting and the good enthralling. They presented programmes that were true, noble, right, pure, lovely, admirable, excellent and worthy of praise.

It was a good land, a shining land, a land of the Book, a land of the Bible. But it was only a dream. Wouldn't it be good if we all had such a dream? Couldn't we pray and live and strive for such a dream? And make that dream a reality? A good land—a *shining* land.

Fellowship

18 LETTER—Fellowship

Dear *Bob,*

You wrote and asked me what 'fellowship' means. Now, as you know, I am no scholar, so I can't go into all the various meanings of the word as it is used in the Scriptures. All I can hope to do is share some of my thoughts and experiences on the subject. I fear 'fellowship' is one of those words which are often misused by Christians.

It is not just friendship or comradeship as some seem to imply. They talk as if having a cup of tea with someone is real fellowship. The truth is, I have often had a cup of tea, even a whole meal with people, and had absolutely nothing in common with them. It seems to me to degrade the word 'fellowship' by applying it to a situation like that. Surely the fellowship we are to enjoy as God's people is deeper than that!

Can I say I had a great time of fellowship, when all we discussed was the weather—or where we were going on holiday? Is it fellowship to have a cup of coffee with someone in the station while waiting for our respective trains?

As I understand it, fellowship involves two factors—sharing and love. Christian fellowship means sharing. We have fellowship because we share the same faith; we are brothers or sisters in the Lord. So we can share at the deepest level a common faith. And we can share with one another what the Lord is doing for us, or how he is testing us. This means we can have fellowship in prayer—even by praying for one another when apart!

Love must also be involved in Christian fellowship. We know the love of God, and of his Son, Jesus Christ, who loved us and gave himself for us. Knowing the love of the Father, we are to have love for all his children. So we have fellowship in love, respecting and sharing with one another.

I think it is important to realise that fellowship is normally a by-product. It is as we do things together, sharing responsibilities and duties, that we find true fellowship. It is then we can appreciate one another's gifts, abilities and personalities. After all, when the Lord sent out his disciples, it was two by two. I am sure they had real fellowship, one with the other, as they shared in the Lord's work.

Fellowship is a rich blessing from God to his children. Nor is that blessing just with one another. We are to have fellowship with God himself. We are sharing his work on earth and are to know his love in our hearts. So our prayer time is to be one of fellowship with God.

Then the benediction, as taught by Paul, asks for the 'fellowship of the Holy Spirit' to be with us. So we are to experience the fellowship of the third person of the Trinity in our daily lives.

I hope this is of some help.

Jim

Part III
LIFE OF THE CHRISTIAN

Doubt

1 INTERVIEW—Thomas

INTERVIEWER: You are Thomas, now known as 'Doubting Thomas'?

THOMAS: Yes, a man makes one mistake and gets labelled for life!

INTERVIEWER: I can appreciate that. You were one of the original twelve followers of Jesus. Indeed you were with him on that last journey to Jerusalem?

THOMAS: Yes, I wanted to go and die with him.

INTERVIEWER: Die with him?

THOMAS: That's what I said when he decided to go back to Jerusalem. With the enemies Jesus had by that time, it was mad to go anywhere near Jerusalem. Most of us were against the idea. But I said, 'Let's go and die with him.' Brave words are easy to speak. But when the time came, I was as cowardly as the rest. Perhaps, in view of my words, *more* cowardly. When the crunch came I did not die—I did not fight—I ran away.

INTERVIEWER: I think we know something of how you feel. But I really want to ask you about the events after Jesus rose from the dead. On that first Sunday when Jesus appeared to the disciples you were not with them, were you?

THOMAS: No.

INTERVIEWER: Where were you?

THOMAS: I was alone—(*hesitates*)—Grief affects people in different ways. Some want to be with others, sharing their sorrow. Some, like me, want to be alone. Alone in their own misery. I just wanted to be on my own, hugging my own sorrow.

INTERVIEWER: I believe the disciples told you they had seen Jesus?

THOMAS: Yes, they told me.

INTERVIEWER: But you did not believe them, did you?

THOMAS: That's right, I didn't believe them. In fact, I *refused* to believe them; refused even to consider the possibility that Jesus was alive. I wanted proof—real proof. So I said: 'Unless I see the nail marks in his hands and put my fingers where the nails were, and put my hand into his side, I will not believe it.'

INTERVIEWER: I must admit that seems a reasonable sort of position to take.

THOMAS: No! It is a totally unreasonable position. It meant I was refusing to consider the possibility of something happening—Jesus rising from the dead. That was a bigoted, narrow-minded viewpoint. But worse than that: Jesus had promised to come back, and I did not believe him. And the disciples were my friends—I knew them and could trust them—but I didn't believe them either. So I refused to believe my Lord, I refused to believe my friends. Surely that's not reasonable, is it?

INTERVIEWER: I see what you mean. However, your doubts were resolved.

THOMAS: Yes, the following Sunday. It had been a terrible week for me. Doubt is the enemy of peace and joy. The other disciples were all so sure but I was lost in a cloud of doubt. I had no faith, no hope. Then Jesus appeared again to the disciples—and this time I was with them.

INTERVIEWER: Did Jesus speak specifically to you?

THOMAS: Yes. He knew of my doubts, my unreasonable demands. So all the stupid words I had spoken he gave back to me. 'Thomas,' he said, 'put your fingers here, see my hands. Reach out your hand and put it into my side. Stop doubting and believe.' There was rebuke in his words, but there was also an ache of love in his voice. He wanted me to believe, to trust him, not to be consumed with the pain of doubt.

INTERVIEWER: Did you do it? Did you touch him?

THOMAS: I had no need to touch him. I was in the presence of the Lord and I knew it. I did the only thing anyone can do when confronted with the living Lord. I fell on my knees and worshipped him, 'My Lord and my God.' I confessed. He was my Lord. He was my God.

INTERVIEWER: Did Jesus say anything else to you?

THOMAS: Yes, he added something for me, for you and for

all time. 'Thomas,' he said, 'because you have seen me you have believed, blessed are those who have not seen and yet have believed.'

2 TESTIMONY—Lost Christian

I remember the church. There is always the church. But it was all long, long ago. A different life. Once it meant something to me. I had almost forgotten. But when I sit and think, it comes back to me. It all comes back to me.

There were church bells, ringing over the town roofs, calling the people to worship. They sounded different then. *Ding-dong. Ding-dong. Come-and wor-ship. Come-and wor-ship.* Of course people went to worship in those days. I remember the crowded pews. Then the glorious hymns that seemed to lift me to the very presence of God.

Of course, there was a God in those days. And prayers that echoed the aches and longing of my heart. Prayers that poured out the thanksgiving that swelled in my breast. Yes, I remember the prayers. Of course, people prayed in those days

Then there were readings from the Bible that seemed to express the majestic language of heaven—the very words of life, promising joy, peace and triumph. Of course, we read the Bible in those days.

Then the words of the preacher—a stirring call to live; to know a higher, more noble life; to rise and follow Christ. To follow Christ the conqueror who would triumph throughout every tribe and tongue and nation. The Christ who would triumph with the puny weapons of love, compassion and

94

humility. The Christ to whom every knee would bow and every tongue confess that he is Lord.

Yes, like a mighty army was the Church of God. But it all seems long, long ago; so far, far away. What has happened to that church? Or dare I ask the question—what has happened to me?

3 TESTIMONY—Family Conversion

A Christian, as I understand it, is someone who believes in the Lord Jesus Christ. We become Christian by faith through the grace of God.

Now this may surprise you, but I can't remember a time when I did not believe, or did not know Jesus as my Saviour and Lord. I was brought up in a Christian home. From my earliest days I was taught the Bible, taught to say my prayers, and taught to see Jesus as my friend, indeed my Saviour. I was taught how he loved me, and even died for me.

I know I had a very simple, childish faith in those days. But didn't the Lord welcome the simplest of faith and didn't he advise us all to become childlike in our faith and love? Certainly as a child I knew nothing about theology, or about the Bible except some of its stories. But even then I knew Jesus was the Son of God who loved me, would be with me, and would forgive me when I did wrong. And I knew I would go to heaven eventually because that is what Jesus promised.

I am older now, maybe many think my faith is still childish. But I prefer to think of it as child*like*. And I am still learning. The Jesus I adored as a little child, I still love and, like

Paul, long to know him better. I want to really grow in grace and knowledge of the truth, and to develop the faith I was taught at my mother's knee.

So I thank God that I was born and brought up in a Christian home, where godly habits were learned, where reading the Bible was seen as a normal activity, where prayers were said every day, and no meal was eaten without first giving thanks. We were taught to confess our sins to the Lord, to be thankful for all his good gifts, and to look upon God as our loving heavenly Father.

Yes, it may seem strange to some people, but I can't remember a time when I did not know Jesus to be my Saviour. I can't recall a time when I did not believe.

4 TESTIMONY—Gradual Conversion

I am a Christian but, to tell the truth, I don't know when I became one! Sometimes I envy those who can tell how they became a Christian at a certain time and place. But I'm a Christian—and all I can tell you is my story.

My parents went occasionally to church, but they left it to me whether I went or not. So, needless to say, I rarely went. But there was a girl in whom I was interested. She worked in a newsagents, and I knew she went to my parents' church. Sometimes I talked to her in the shop, but it was difficult because there were always people coming in for papers, cigarettes or something. But one morning she told me about the Youth Fellowship they had started and invited me to go.

So the next Sunday I went to the evening service prior to the Youth Fellowship. It was then I noticed the girl coming in hand in hand with another boy, and I saw my hopes of romance disappear. It was an old minister who was taking the service and I can truthfully say it was boring from beginning to end. In his sermon he just went on and on. I decided to get out of the church quickly and forget about the Youth Fellowship, and the girl.

The old minister was at the door shaking hands with those that were there. He shook my hand and asked my name. 'Andrew,' I said, trying to get away. I was conscious of the girl and her boyfriend immediately behind me. They would want me to go to the Youth Fellowship.

The old minister patted me on the shoulder and said, '*Andrew*, eh? *One of his disciples.*'

'*One of his disciples*'—that was all he said, but the words echoed through my mind as I hurried away. I heard the girl call my name, but I didn't stop.

'*One of his disciples*'—the phrase seemed to have a ring about it, a challenge. I could not get it out of my mind. There seemed to be something gloriously noble about it.

'*One of his disciples*'—there was something frightening about it too. It sounded so old-fashioned. As I walked home that night I kept hearing those words over and over again. I knew nothing about Andrew, the disciple. After getting home I was determined to forget the words of the doddering old minister.

In the days that followed I could not forget the words so easily. I found myself wondering who Andrew really was. One night I even tried to look it up in the Bible to see if I could find out something about him. But I didn't know where to look and kept getting long lists of unpronounceable names, or passages about Moses and Jeremiah—everything but Andrew. I asked my mother where Andrew was in the Bible, but she laughed and said, 'You were called after your grandfather.'

'*Andrew—one of his disciples.*' The words kept coming back to me, and it was as if I should be one of his disciples. But how could I be? I knew nothing about the Bible or Jesus.

I went back to church the following Sunday, hoping the minister would preach about Andrew. But it was all about Moses. The really interesting part was the Bible reading, which he said was in the New Testament. It was in John's Gospel, and finally Andrew was mentioned.

I took out my diary and took a note of the reading. I wanted to read about Andrew when I got home.

That afternoon I sat in my room and read right through John's Gospel. I actually found it interesting. But what really surprised me was the more I read about Andrew, the more I became interested in Jesus. He must have been a fascinating character. No wonder Andrew became one of his disciples.

That week I read through the four Gospels. Some scarcely mention Andrew, but that didn't matter now. I even started to pray. I don't think I knew what was happening to me. At work I found when someone used the name of Jesus as an oath—as I had often done—it troubled me. It seemed so disrespectful to the Jesus I was reading about.

Maybe, at that point, I should have gone to the minister to discuss things. But the thought never entered my head. I just kept on reading the Bible and trying to understand it for myself. It was changing me, although I don't think I was aware of it myself.

The crunch came about a month later when someone swore at work, using the name of Jesus in a scathing, mocking way. 'Must you do that?' I asked. The man looked at me and said, 'Are you a Christian?' 'Yes,' I answered, and it was as big a shock to me as it was to him. I was Andrew, one of his disciples and how could I disown my Lord? It was that night I went to see the minister to say I wanted to join the church.

I am a Christian—but I don't really know exactly when

it happened. The important thing is that it *did* happen. Maybe I am not very good or faithful to my Lord, but I am thankful that I am now 'one of his disciples'.

5 TESTIMONY—Sudden Conversion

I am a Christian—and it came about in a most remarkable way. I had been a member of the church, indeed an elder, for many years. And then I became a Christian.

I know that sounds strange—almost unbelievable. In fact it is almost unbelievable to me. But it's the truth. And it came about this way.

It was a Communion Service. We were singing the Communion hymn when it happened. The hymn was 'When I survey the wondrous cross'. I always liked that hymn—it has good words and a good tune. I started to sing, as lustily as ever. Then suddenly, as if they were exploding in my mind, I began to experience the actual words I was singing. It was as if I had never heard them before.

There was a sudden stab of guilt. I realised that my richest gain I had not counted but loss, and certainly had never poured contempt on all my pride. In some strange way I became aware that I had really been proud of myself and my status. I prided myself in being a good church member and a conscientious elder. I liked being looked up to and respected as a good churchman. I had done and said all the right things. I felt I had a lot for which to be proud. I was a respectable churchman.

With the sudden sense of guilt there came an intense feeling of sorrow ... regret ... repentance. In my mind's eye I did indeed see from his head, his hands, his feet, sorrow and love flow mingled down. In a way I had never known before, I realised that Jesus Christ loved me, and died for me. It was my sins—my self-righteousness—my pride that nailed him to that terrible cross.

There was guilt—repentance—then acceptance. I truly wanted to give my soul, my life, my all. I, a hypocrite, a self-righteous sinner could only throw myself at his feet and beg for mercy and grace. At that moment, I believe, I became a Christian—one of the lost who was found by the Good Shepherd, the one who gave his life for lost sheep like me.

I realised that, up to that moment, I had really trusted in my own merits. I had thought I was a good man, a faithful churchman, a good religious person. Singing that hymn I came to know the sad fact—I was simply a sinner. Maybe a respectable sinner—a religious sinner—because I had clung to the vain things that really charmed me most. I had trusted them to make me acceptable to God. I had not realised that it is only through the blood of Christ that we are forgiven and restored.

Maybe it is a strange story. But all I know is that suddenly, in singing that hymn, I threw overboard my self-righteousness and pride. I trusted Jesus alone for my salvation.

Forgiveness

6 INTERVIEW—Peter

INTERVIEWER: You are Peter. You have the reputation of being a strong man, a leader of men.

PETER: Maybe, but never forget that even the strongest can break. I said I would die for Jesus, but ended up denying him.

INTERVIEWER: Would you like to tell us about it?

PETER: It's a sorry tale. Jesus told us he was going away, and that we would all let him down. I thought I wouldn't. And I meant it. 'Will you really lay down your life for me, Peter,' he said. 'I tell you the truth. Before the cock crows you will disown me three times.' I didn't believe him.

INTERVIEWER: But what Jesus said came true, didn't it?

PETER: Yes. It was like a nightmare—Gethsemane! There were soldiers and Temple guards and an angry mob. Judas was leading them. Jesus was arrested. I grabbed a sword and tried to fight but Jesus rebuked me. We all ran away. After a while John and I came back to find out what was happening. A servant girl recognised me. 'You are one of them,' she said. And I denied it. I was afraid of the soldiers and the bloodthirsty mob. Three times I denied knowing Jesus. The third time with oaths and curses.

INTERVIEWER: It must have been a terrifying situation for

you. So perhaps under the circumstances it was understandable.

PETER: He knew me better than I knew myself. Then two things happened that really shattered me ....

INTERVIEWER: What were they?

PETER: The cock crowed. And Jesus was brought out. He looked at me. I will never forget that look. There was disappointment in his eyes. I had let him down. But there was also love. It was that which really broke my heart. He loved me and I had denied him. I could only weep with a heart that was breaking. I was filled with remorse and guilt and shame.

INTERVIEWER: But things are different now?

PETER: Yes.

INTERVIEWER: What's the difference?

PETER: He is risen—and I'm forgiven.

INTERVIEWER: Tell us about it. I believe you were among the first at the tomb that Sunday morning?

PETER: The women were first. They came back and told us the tomb was empty. John and I ran to the tomb. John got there first and stood outside. I rushed straight in. The grave-clothes were lying where the body had been—just as if he had come out through them.

INTERVIEWER: Did you believe then that Jesus had risen?

PETER: I didn't know what to believe. I didn't know what was going on.

INTERVIEWER: So when did you first realise he had risen?

PETER: He appeared to us in Jerusalem that first Sunday. But it is the Galilean meeting I remember best. We had gone back to Galilee as he had told us. But we didn't know what to do. I don't like waiting. I don't have the patience. I suggested we go fishing. It was a dismal night. We caught nothing. By the morning we were tired and depressed.

INTERVIEWER: But what about Jesus? I thought you said you met him in Galilee?

PETER: We did. It was as we were rowing towards the shore. We saw a man standing on the beach. 'Friends, have you caught any fish?' he asked. 'No!' we shouted back. He told us to cast our net on the right side of the boat. We did—and got a great catch of fish. I was busy helping to haul in the fish when John shouted, 'It's the Lord!' I immediately dived into the water and swam and waded ashore. It was Jesus—and you'll never guess what he was doing.

INTERVIEWER: What was he doing?

PETER: Getting a good fire going and cooking fish for our breakfast. Can you imagine it? The risen Lord of Glory kindling a fire, cooking fish, preparing breakfast for us.

INTERVIEWER: Was it then you had a talk with him?

PETER: Yes—or rather he had a talk with me. He asked me if I loved him. *I did love him.* Three times he asked me that question: 'Peter, do you love me?' Three times I answered 'Yes!' He knew that I loved him.

INTERVIEWER: You say he asked three times if you loved him? Why do you think he asked *three* times?

PETER: Three times I denied him—and three times he made me confess my love for him. It was as if he was giving me the opportunity to wipe out the memory of my denials.

INTERVIEWER: That's interesting. Jesus gave you the chance to cancel out your denials?

PETER: Yes—but it was more than that. It was not just for-giveness for the past—there was a commission for the future. He told me to feed his lambs and sheep. I will try to do that. I will work to establish his Kingdom and build his church on earth. No longer in my own strength, but by his strength and grace. I have learned not to trust my own strength.

7 DIALOGUE—'I don't sin!'

ONE: You know, I don't like all this talk of sin. It's as though we're all a bunch of terrible sinners.

TWO: Don't you think we are?

ONE: Well, I'm not really a sinner!

TWO: But the Bible says that we have all sinned.

ONE: Are you trying to say I'm a sinner?

TWO: No! It's the Bible that says it.

ONE: But I mean—I've never murdered anyone. I don't go around causing bother and hating people. I've lived a decent life and no one can accuse me of anything really bad.

TWO: But sin isn't just big bad things.

ONE: What is it then?

TWO: There are two types of sin—omission and commission.

ONE: What do you mean?

TWO: Sins of omission are *not* doing the things we should do—and sins of commission are *deliberately doing* the things we shouldn't do.

ONE: Well, I've never done anything I shouldn't do!

TWO: That sounds a little bit like self-righteousness. Isn't that a sin?

ONE: Well, none of us are perfect.

TWO: That means you are sinner then, doesn't it?

ONE: I'm not so sure. As far as I'm concerned sinners are

really wicked people. That's one thing I can take pride in—I'm not really a bad person.

TWO: Pride—well, that's also a sin!

ONE: You are just trying to trap me.

TWO: No, not at all—but sometimes I think that the really troublesome sins are those we just don't think about, the ones we see no harm in.

ONE: Such as?

TWO: Samuel in the Bible says, 'Forbid that I should sin by not praying for you.' Maybe we sin by not praying for one another.

ONE: I don't think that's a sin.

TWO: That's *your* opinion—not God's.

ONE: You mean I should start praying for others, especially some folk I know?

TWO: How about 'Taking the Lord's name in vain'?

ONE: Oh, I never swear. No one has ever heard me swearing!

TWO: But we can do it by singing hymns that we don't really mean.

ONE: What do you mean? How can we do that? I like a good sing-song.

TWO: 'Take my life and let it be, consecrated Lord to thee ...
Take my silver and my gold, not a mite would I withhold.'
'When I survey the wondrous cross on which the Prince of
glory died ... my richest gain I count but loss and pour
contempt on all my pride.' Sometimes, singing those sort
of hymns, I wonder if I really mean what I am singing.

ONE: Oh—I just like singing.

TWO: But singing words like those, and not really meaning
them—am I not telling lies, and taking God's name in
vain?

ONE: I look on sin as doing harm to someone else.

TWO: But sin is against God, not man.

ONE: I think you are making it too complicated. I mean sin
is just killing, stealing ....

TWO: Have you never pinched a pencil, ruler, paper, paper-
clip from your office?

ONE: That's different. They're just lying around. It's not
really stealing. It's not really breaking the law.

TWO: Jesus told us what the law really was—'You shall love
the Lord your God with all your heart, soul, mind and
body, and your neighbour as yourself.'

ONE: Yes, I think I remember that.

TWO: Do you really love God with all your heart, soul, mind
and body?

ONE: Well, that's a bit fanatical, isn't it?

TWO: And do you love your neighbour as yourself?

ONE: You should see some of the neighbours I've got!

TWO: And you say you keep the law?

ONE: Well—anyway—doesn't God forgive our sins?

TWO: But how can we be forgiven if we say we haven't sinned?

ONE: I don't know. Maybe I'm not as good as I thought I was.

TWO: Well, none of us are!

(Scripts 8-10 tell the story of Elijah, exploring trust in God and also distrust.)

Trust

8 INTERVIEW—Widow of Zarephath (*1 Kings 17*)

INTERVIEWER: I understand that you know Elijah—this troublemaker in Israel.

WIDOW: He's not a troublemaker. He's a man of God.

INTERVIEWER: King Ahab says he is a troublemaker. Anyway, how well do you know Elijah?

WIDOW: He lodged with me for some time.

INTERVIEWER: He actually stayed with you? When did you meet him?

WIDOW: It was the worst time, the time of the drought. There was no rain and the very river beds dried up. It was one day as I was going out to gather sticks to light a fire. I had only a little flour and oil in the house and I was going to light a fire to make our last meal. After that, my son and I would die, for we had no more food at all. Then Elijah appeared.

INTERVIEWER: Did you recognise who he was?

WIDOW: No—not to begin with.

INTERVIEWER: What did he want?

WIDOW: He asked me for a drink of water. Very polite, he was. We didn't have much water, but how can you refuse a stranger a drink? I was just turning to get him some water when he added, 'And bring me a piece of bread.'

INTERVIEWER: He seemed to know what he wanted. Did he not realise how poor you were—that you had virtually no food? Did you give him what he wanted?

WIDOW: Not at first. I told him I didn't have any bread. I had only a handful of flour and a little oil in a jar. So I apologised. I told him how poor we were.

INTERVIEWER: How did he respond to your plight?

WIDOW: He told me not to be afraid. It wasn't just his words, but the way he spoke them. I didn't know, but I felt then that this was a man of God—a man who trusts God and will never be let down by God. Then he said a remarkable thing. I don't think I really took it in, but somehow or other I knew what he said would come true.

INTERVIEWER: Yes—but what did he say?

WIDOW: He said—and these are his exact words, I will never forget them—'This is what the Lord, the God of Israel says: *The jar of flour will not be used up and the jar of oil will not run dry until the day the Lord gives rain on the land.*'

INTERVIEWER: And you believed that! You believed that God would work a miracle. Is that what you are saying?

WIDOW: Yes. I mean, it was as if I had heard the Lord God of Israel speaking to me. He used the voice of Elijah, but it was God who was speaking. Yes—I believed it. Should we not believe the Lord God when he speaks?

INTERVIEWER: Are you trying to tell us that from then onwards your flour and oil never went down until the drought ended?

WIDOW: I am not *trying* to tell you—I am *telling* you. It never went down. That's a fact. I took Elijah into my home, I made him a meal, and from then onwards the level of the flour and oil did not go down even though I kept using it.

INTERVIEWER: But that's impossible!

WIDOW: With God? Is it impossible for the God who made the heavens and the earth to do that?

INTERVIEWER: So you are telling us that Elijah performed this miracle?

WIDOW: Elijah performed no miracle. It was God. Only God can perform miracles.

INTERVIEWER: Let's forget this talk of miracles. Elijah stayed with you and you must have got to know him. What did you think of him?

WIDOW: He was a man of God. A prophet of the Most High. What else could I think?

INTERVIEWER: Because of the flour and oil that never went down?

WIDOW: And because of my son.

INTERVIEWER: Your son? What about your son?

WIDOW: My son—my only son—became ill. I did all I could —nursed him, prayed for him, cared for him—but he grew worse. Then he died.

INTERVIEWER: So your great Elijah couldn't save him?

WIDOW: May God forgive me, but in my grief for the loss of my son I was angry with Elijah. I blamed him for his death, forgetting it is God alone who gives life and takes life away.

INTERVIEWER: That was a tragedy. How did Elijah take it?

WIDOW: He was not annoyed at my anger. I think he understood it. 'Give me your son,' he said, and took the lifeless body of my son in his arms. He carried my boy up to his room and laid him on the bed. Then he prayed, cried out in anguish to the Lord. I remember his words. 'O Lord my God, have you brought tragedy upon the widow I am staying with by causing her son to die?' Then he stretched out three times on top of my boy and cried—'O Lord my God, let the boy's life return to him.'

INTERVIEWER: Your son came back to life just because Elijah prayed for him. Is that what you are telling us?

WIDOW: Yes. Although I was downstairs—alone with my grief—I heard his voice. Then a great sigh as of someone waking from sleep. Elijah came down into my room. He was carrying my boy in his arms. And the boy ... the boy was *breathing*. 'Look,' said Elijah, 'your son is *alive*.' It was true.

INTERVIEWER: It seems a remarkable story. But …

WIDOW: Doesn't that show that Elijah was a man of God—a prophet of the Almighty? A man who trusted God, and helped me to trust also.

9 INTERVIEW—Man at Carmel (1 Kings 18)

INTERVIEWER: Elijah left the widow of Zarephath and confronted King Ahab. He threw out a challenge to the King and all Israel. It was to be a contest at Mount Carmel between Baal and the Lord God. We have here one of the spectators who witnessed that event.

You were one of the crowd at Mount Carmel?

MAN: Yes, I was. It was a real showdown. It was exciting, I can tell you.

INTERVIEWER: Whose side were you on?

MAN: You mean between Baal and God? Well, it's not as simple as all that. You see, I quite liked Ahab and his ways. Baal offered you a good life—you could enjoy yourself. Ahab knew all about that. Take the easy way and be happy. That was Ahab's way. Of course he had Jezebel. She was some woman, I can tell you! She knew how to enjoy herself and get her own way.

INTERVIEWER: So you didn't like Elijah?

MAN: Who would? I mean he was religious, a real killjoy— always on about commandments and obeying God.

INTERVIEWER: Do you think Elijah is a prophet?

MAN: A prophet? The country is full of prophets. Somebody told me Baal had 450 prophets. Elijah is only one more. Of course he is different. He opposed the prophets of Baal at Mount Carmel.

INTERVIEWER: So what happened at Mount Carmel?

MAN: It was amazing, I'll say that. Really exciting! There were to be two sacrifices. Altars were built—sort of bonfires, you know. One for Baal and one for the Lord God. A bull was to be sacrificed and put on the altar of Baal. Then the prophets were to ask Baal to send down fire from heaven to burn up and accept the sacrifice.

INTERVIEWER: And did fire come down from Baal and burn up the sacrifice?

MAN: No. The prophets of Baal prayed and shouted and danced all round the altar, but nothing happened. No fire! It went on for hours. But nobody left. In a way it was quite entertaining.

INTERVIEWER: What do you mean—entertaining?

MAN: Elijah started to mock them. I didn't think Elijah had
    any sense of humour, but he had us all laughing at his
    words and the antics of the prophets. He kept taunting
    them: 'Maybe you should shout louder. Maybe Baal is
    busy elsewhere. Maybe he's away somewhere. Maybe
    he's asleep—try and waken him.' It was great!

INTERVIEWER: But no fire came?

MAN: No! No fire came. In a way I felt sorry for those
    prophets. They ended up completely tired out.

INTERVIEWER: Well, it would have been a real miracle if fire
    had come down and burned up the sacrifice. But what
    about Elijah?

MAN: I tell you he really mocked the prophets. He had a
    real sense of the dramatic. Do you know what he did?

INTERVIEWER: No—that is what we would like to find out.
    Could you go on? What did he do?

MAN: He built his altar—all the wood and everything. Then
    he poured water over it. He even got others to help him
    pour big barrels of water over the wood. It must have
    been soaking. And it seemed such a waste. It hadn't rained
    for three years, you know.

INTERVIEWER: So—what happened?

MAN: I tell you I have never seen anything like it in my life.
    Elijah prayed, and then suddenly—*whoosh*—the whole
    thing burst into flames. Some say they saw fire coming
    down from heaven. I don't know, but suddenly every-

thing was aflame, blazing fiercely. Everything was burned up—bull, wood, stones—even the water. I have never seen anything like it in my whole life!

INTERVIEWER: So fire did fall on Elijah's sacrifice. That must have shaken you all. How did the crowd react?

MAN: What could we do? I was just like the rest. I fell down on my knees—who wouldn't? If God could do that to a soaking altar, what could he do to us if he wanted? There could be no doubt—Baal was an illusion. Only the Lord is God.

INTERVIEWER: So you believe in the Lord now, do you? You have decided to trust him?

MAN: Well, I wouldn't say that. But what happened at Mount Carmel makes you think. It makes you think, I can tell you!

10 INTERVIEW—Elijah's Servant

INTERVIEWER: Let us turn to one who probably knew more about Elijah than anyone—his servant. What would you say about Elijah?

SERVANT: He had the highest status of all men. He was a man of God, a man of faith, a prophet of God—a man to whom God spoke, and through whom God worked.

INTERVIEWER: Of course, as his servant and friend, you would be expected to say things like that.

SERVANT: But how can anyone doubt it? He fed the hungry at Zarephath—raised the dead—and the events at Mount Carmel proved that God was with him.

INTERVIEWER: Give me your thoughts on Carmel. Why do you think Elijah arranged that confrontation?

SERVANT: It was a challenge—not just to the King or the priests of Baal. It was a challenge to the people. They were so vague about what they believed. First they trusted one thing, and then another. So Elijah challenged them to make up their minds who they would trust. As he put it—'How long will you waver between two opinions. If the Lord is God, follow him: if Baal is God, follow him.'

INTERVIEWER: That was quite a challenge. Could you go on?

SERVANT: Yes, there was Elijah—a lone prophet of the Lord against 450 prophets of Baal. It shows that the majority are not always right.

INTERVIEWER: But the majority changed their minds, didn't they?

SERVANT: Not at the beginning. But with their own eyes they saw the failure of Baal. False prophets pleading with a false god brought no results. In spite of their frenzied praying, their sincerity, their commitment—Baal could not help. There is only one God—the Lord.

INTERVIEWER: I believe Elijah built an altar and soaked it in water. Can you tell us a bit more?

SERVANT: Yes—he had to rebuild the altar of the Lord. That showed how far the people had departed from the faith of their fathers. The altar built by their fathers to worship the Lord lay in ruins.

INTERVIEWER: So you are saying that Elijah rebuilt the altar?

SERVANT: Yes—and remember Elijah poured water over it. Four large barrels of water were poured over the wood on the altar. Three times he ordered that to be done. That makes twelve full barrels of water! He wanted the wavering people to see the power of the Lord—who can make even water burn.

INTERVIEWER: Did he then command God to send down fire?

SERVANT: Command! Can a creature dictate to the Creator? A servant to his master? No! He prayed. Elijah prayed: 'Lord, God of Abraham, Isaac and Israel, let it be known today that you are God in Israel and that I am your servant and have done all these things at your command. Answer me, O Lord, answer me, so that these people will know that you, O Lord, are God, and that you are turning their hearts back again.' Then the fire fell.

INTERVIEWER: Was it not simply a piece of trickery on Elijah's part?

SERVANT: Trickery? Don't be silly! Can God not send fire from heaven? He can and he did. I saw it—we all saw it.

The fire came and burned up the sacrifice, the wood, the stones, and the very earth on which it was built. Even the water in the trenches around the altar boiled away into nothing.

INTERVIEWER: I believe at this point the crowd all acknowledged God.

SERVANT: They had to. They fell on their faces crying, 'The Lord, he is God. The Lord, he is God.' How could anyone doubt when they had seen the works of the Lord before their very eyes?

INTERVIEWER: Finally—can I ask you about the drought? It was about then the rains came. Can you cast any light on this for us?

SERVANT: Elijah took me up to the top of Mount Carmel. He asked me to look over towards the sea for the coming rain. I looked, but saw nothing but a cloudless sky. I told him so. Seven times he asked me to go and look while he was quiet in prayer. Then the seventh time I had to report: 'I see a cloud as small as a man's hand arising from the sea.' The sky grew darker. It grew black as the wind rose and then came the rain—heavy, torrential rain. God watered the parched land of Israel.

Hope

11 INTERVIEW—John on Patmos

INTERVIEWER: John, you are now an old man. As a young man you were one of the witnesses to the resurrection of Jesus. But that was a long time ago—something like sixty years. Paul, in one of his letters, claims to have seen him since, and that he ....

JOHN: (*Interrupts*) I too have seen him.

INTERVIEWER: Yes, I know you saw him once, a long time ago.

JOHN: I didn't see him *once*. I saw him many times.

INTERVIEWER: Yes, but that was a long time ago.

JOHN: I'm not talking about a long time ago.

INTERVIEWER: You mean you have seen Jesus since those early days?

JOHN: Yes.

INTERVIEWER: Where did you see him?

JOHN: On Patmos. You know I was exiled there for the faith? Exiled on the Island of Patmos.

INTERVIEWER: And you saw Jesus there?

120

JOHN: Yes. It was on a Sunday morning—the Lord's day. I was at worship—alone—but I was joined in spirit with all the Lord's people, worshipping the eternal God and his beloved Son. Then it happened.

INTERVIEWER: What happened?

JOHN: I saw Jesus.

INTERVIEWER: Could you tell us about it?

JOHN: I heard a voice behind me. A voice like no other voice on earth. A voice that penetrated my mind and thrilled my heart like a trumpet call. It was a voice of music—I've never heard anything on earth like it.

INTERVIEWER: That must have been quite an experience. What did the voice say?

JOHN: 'Write—write down what I will show you and send it to the churches in Asia.' I turned round to see the owner of the voice that spoke to me in tones of heavenly music. Then I saw him. I saw the Lord.

INTERVIEWER: Was he as you remembered him? Had he changed in any way? What did he look like?

JOHN: Oh—it would take a poet, a miracle-worker with words, to describe what I saw. The Son of Man stood there, yet he was like no man on earth. It was as if he was bathed in light, surrounded by candlesticks illuminating only him. Yet he *was* the light. A figure of light—colour, beauty, glory, majesty beyond all imagination. His face was like the sun shining in all its brilliance. His eyes were dazzling with fire and penetrating like a sword so that he was looking into my heart, soul and mind.

INTERVIEWER: Are you sure this was Jesus you were seeing?

JOHN: Yes! During his days on earth we saw him on the Mount of Transfiguration, where heaven shone through his earthly flesh and we saw something of his glory. But even that was only a shadow of the heavenly Lord I met on Patmos. When I saw him I fell at his feet as dead.

INTERVIEWER: Are you sure this really happened—that it wasn't some sort of mystical experience?

JOHN: Oh, it happened all right. He leaned down, put his hand on my shoulder to lift me up, and said: 'Do not be afraid.' Those old beloved and familiar words—'*Do not be afraid.*' How often we had heard them during his earthly life. He spoke them to me that morning on Patmos. Gave me the same assurance. He was there. There was no need to doubt. It was then he asked me to write certain things.

INTERVIEWER: What was it that you had to write down?

JOHN: You can read it in the Book of Revelation as you call it. I was called to write down all the things he told me; all the things he showed me. It is all a reaffirmation of what the rest of the Scriptures foretell and proclaim. The Lord and his Christ shall reign for ever and ever.

INTERVIEWER: Stephen saw him. Paul saw him. You saw him. Do you think anyone else will see him?

JOHN: Yes, all eyes will see him. Jesus shall return. He will come back to this sad earth. Not as a suffering servant. Not to be spat upon, mocked and crucified. He will come back in majesty and glory with all the armies of heaven escorting him to take his rightful place on earth.

INTERVIEWER: Do you really believe this?

JOHN: Yes! And he will indeed be King of kings, and Lord of lords. He will reign with justice and righteousness— and of his Kingdom there will be no end.

12 LETTER—'I saw Jesus!'

Dear *Marcus,*

You ask me to tell you something about this Jesus you have heard about. Yes, I know him, but am not counted among his followers. I really am fascinated by him.

You say that you heard he was a very loving person. He is, but I wonder if 'loving' is a strong enough word for what he is and does. It is as if he takes the concept of love and moves it into a higher plane.

The first time I heard him he was preaching on a mountainside, and among the startling things he said was— 'Love not just your neighbour, but your enemies'! Surely an astonishing ideal!

Certainly he loved his neighbours—and he defined our neighbour as anyone in need of help. Day after day I saw him helping, loving people. Lepers came to him. His face shone with compassion, and I even saw him touch, actually

123

embrace, a leper. Isn't such a thing unthinkable? But in love he gave them what they had been denied for so long—a human touch. Not only that, but he healed them! I found it an awesome sight.

One day a leader of the Jews, Jairus by name, came to Jesus because his little girl was dying. In love Jesus immediately set out to go to the little girl. As always, a crowd followed him.

Suddenly, Jesus stopped and asked, 'Who touched me?' Even his disciples were bewildered—the crowd was pressing in on him, pushing to get a closer view, and Jesus asked, 'Who touched me?'

But a woman, who had suffered from a long illness, confessed that she had touched him, hoping to be healed. She was healed. Jesus was all compassion with her. It was as if he had forgotten poor Jairus standing there, still worried sick about his daughter. But Jesus, in love, has time for those who need him. He spoke to the woman, and then went on with Jairus.

But, by that time, word came that the little girl had died. Jesus comforted Jairus by assuring him that it would be all right. It was! The little girl was dead—but Jesus raised her from the dead! What kind of man can do that?

Even for those who did not agree with him, Jesus has nothing but love. A rich young ruler came to him asking for eternal life. Jesus knew the man was rooted in this world's riches, and told him to give them all up and follow him. Of course, like most sensible people, the young man left Jesus and went back to his rich lifestyle. But I shall never forget the look on Jesus' face as he saw the young man go away. His face showed his disappointment and shone with love for that poor young man. There was pity, compassion, tenderness and love on the face of Jesus as he saw that young man leave.

Love, of course, can be painful, as the incident with the rich young ruler showed. The pain of love showed in the tears of Jesus at the graveside of his friend Lazarus. He wept as many of us have wept at the grave of a loved one. But the astonishing thing is that Jesus *wept*, although he must have known he could—and *would*—bring Lazarus back to life again. I think he was weeping and sobbing at the pain and horror of death.

Then again, I saw him weeping over the city of Jerusalem, the city he knew would reject him. He wanted Jerusalem to know his peace and his love. But the city would not.

Yes, you are right Marcus, they crucified him. But even here he was love personified. As they nailed him to the cross he prayed an almost unbelievable prayer. He prayed to his God, 'Father, forgive them, they do not know what they are doing.' Praying for your murderers even as they are in the act of murdering you! What an astonishing man this was. How could anyone love like that? But he did.

Simon

13 LETTER—What is Love?

Dear *Jim*,

You write saying that you are puzzled by the emphasis on love in your new-found faith in Christ. The Christian religion is certainly a religion of love. Jesus himself summed up the whole law as loving God with all our being, and loving our neighbour.

You ask, 'How can I love people I don't even like?' I know

this puzzles many and, indeed, troubled me at one time. The problem is that the concept of love has been hijacked by the Romantic poets, Hollywood and the Pop culture. They have reduced love to a mere emotion—a feeling. They make it appear to be a sort of passion that grips and controls the heart, a tender sensation that makes us want somebody.

But the biblical love is not like that. After all, we are commanded to love. Would God command us to manufacture emotions, when he knows we cannot conjure up feelings at will? Feelings are emotional responses. We instinctively like or dislike something or someone. In some ways these are beyond our mental control.

But we are commanded to love. That is, to exercise our will in *doing* something, rather than merely *feeling* something.

Jesus said, 'If you love me, obey my commandments.' So if we want to show our love for the Lord, we don't try to get warm feelings in our hearts—we simply do what he wants us to do! So to love our neighbours we should be ever ready to help them. It's what we *do* that matters, not what we *feel*.

I think it was Martin Luther who said something like, 'I'm glad God commanded us to *love* our neighbours—not to *like* them.' I appreciate that. So don't worry about liking or disliking people—love them. Recognise them as creatures bearing God's image, lost sinners for whom Christ died. And while they may not be adorable, likable or endearing, pray for them and be ready to help them.

When Jesus was being crucified, did he like the men who were ruthlessly nailing him to the cross? Certainly, he loved them—praying for their forgiveness.

Of course this business of loving even the unlovable is difficult. The Christian life is hard and we can never, this side of heaven, love the way our Lord loved. But we have to work at it. Like all exercises, physical, mental or spiritual, the more we do it the easier it becomes. Love is expressed in action.

One other thought. I think I can say that I love all God's people. Where a man or woman bows the knee to Jesus, acknowledging him as Saviour and Lord—then I have a brother or sister. I love them because I love the same Lord, and have the same Father in heaven. But I cannot say I like them all. I don't even *know* them all—how can I like someone I don't know?

I hope this helps you.

Frank

Discipleship

14 INTERVIEW—Mary on Stephen's Death

INTERVIEWER: The Christian life is often difficult. Discipleship is not easy. Stephen was the first follower of Jesus to die for his faith. Many saw him die. Among them Mary.

Mary, you knew Stephen?

MARY: Yes, that's right.

INTERVIEWER: Was he an important follower of Jesus?

MARY: All who belong to Jesus are important.

INTERVIEWER: What I mean is, he wasn't an original disciple, was he?

MARY: He wasn't one of the Apostles, if that's what you mean. He was a Deacon. The Apostles couldn't do all the work—the practical caring as well as the preaching and teaching—so they appointed seven Deacons to help. Men of spiritual insight and wisdom. Stephen was one of them.

INTERVIEWER: So he was a practical man, one who looked after the widows and the poor among the believers?

MARY: Yes, but he was more than just a practical man. God had given him preaching abilities and he performed wonders and miracles. He was a fearless and brilliant defender of the faith.

INTERVIEWER: How did he come to be arrested?

MARY: Because those who are against our Lord Jesus Christ could not stand against Stephen's wisdom and debating power. And they dragged him before the Jewish Council.

INTERVIEWER: So there must have been some sort of case against him. There was a formal trial, I believe?

MARY: That's what they called it. But it was like the trial of the Lord. They were not interested in evidence or truth, only in condemnation and conviction. They had lying witnesses and ended by appealing to the mob, not justice.

INTERVIEWER: But surely Stephen spoke up to defend himself?

MARY: Oh you should have seen him! He stood there before his accusers and his face shone like an angel's. Truly the Lord was with him.

INTERVIEWER: But what did he say?

MARY: Luke has written it down for us. You can read it in his book. Stephen was truly inspired. He told those people their own history. Abraham, Joseph, Moses—all the great leaders and prophets God had sent. But they were always a disobedient people, continually turning away from the Living God to serve false gods. Stephen told of the promises of God, which they had ignored or forgotten. Their fathers had murdered those who promised the coming of God's Righteous One. And when he had come in Jesus Christ—they murdered him.

INTERVIEWER: That sounds as though Stephen was really attacking his accusers, instead of defending himself!

MARY: Yes, *exactly.*

INTERVIEWER: What was the verdict? What did they do?

MARY: They handed him over to the mob. Just as they did with our Lord. They let the mob take over in place of justice.

INTERVIEWER: So Stephen was stoned to death?

MARY: Yes, even though it was against the law of Rome; even against their own law. But they let the mob drag Stephen away to be stoned—(*pause*)—and then, somehow, the whole scene became, well—inspiring.

INTERVIEWER: *Inspiring?* A man being brutally stoned to death?

MARY: Stephen stood there. Even before the first stone was thrown, his face shone as he looked upwards. He was looking beyond the horrors of this world. It was as if the heavens were open and he was looking into glory itself. As indeed he was. 'Look,' he cried, 'I see the heavens open and the Son of Man standing at the right hand of God.' He saw the risen, glorified Lord.

INTERVIEWER: What happened then?

MARY: The mob went berserk. They were incensed, devilish in their hate and anger. A hating mob is a frightening thing. But Stephen wasn't afraid.

INTERVIEWER: How do you know he wasn't afraid?

MARY: He prayed. Even as the stones began to fly, he committed himself to his Lord. 'Lord Jesus, receive my spirit,' he prayed. Then as his blood flowed, and the pain engulfed him, he added another prayer: 'Lord, do not hold this sin against them.' Wasn't that inspiring? Like his Lord before him, he prayed for his murderers. We all heard it. Even Saul.

INTERVIEWER: Saul?

MARY: Saul, the Pharisee, was standing nearby watching and listening. He held the cloaks of those who were stoning Stephen.

INTERVIEWER: So Stephen's dead?

MARY: Dead—yes. Well, no, we don't use that word. He only fell asleep. He will wake up one day, his body resurrected to life as the Lord of Life has promised.

15 DREAM—Vows of Membership

NARRATOR: It was not so much a dream, more of a nightmare. It happened in the grey twilight world between sleep and consciousness. I had gone to bed in a glow of self-righteousness, pleased with myself after a good day. That day I had been to church twice, one of the few times when I had gone to both morning and evening services.

There had been a choir taking the evening service and, being fond of music, I went back at night. I had found it an uplifting service, and happily made my way home, contented with life.

Then, lying happily in bed, drifting off to sleep, it happened. A strange dream that merged into a nightmare.

I was in a room, a hall, I'm not sure. Everything was so shadowy I could only see vague figures sitting around. My hands were gripping a brass rail and I seemed to be standing in a sort of wooden box whose sides reached my waist. With a shock I realised I stood in a dock, facing a richly robed judge. His face was in shadows, but I saw the hint of rich purple on his robes.

Then a man, sitting near the Judge, stood up, and his voice echoed in my ears. Shadows gathered so that I could no longer see the speaker, my accuser. I could only hear the voice.

ACCUSER: My Lord, the accused standing before you is charged with deliberately breaking his vows. He made promises he does not keep, pledges he breaks, undertakings he has not fulfilled. He is a breaker of vows. He made four vows.

He was asked: *'Do you repent of your sin and profess your faith in God?'* To that he answered yes. I do not know the state of his mind or understanding when he willingly took that vow before God and the gathered congregation. Only your Lordship knew what was in his heart and mind.

But, my Lord, did he really repent of his sins? Repent, if I may simplify the word, means being sorry and doing something about it. I must query whether he was truly sorry, and whether he has done anything about it. Has he fought against the sin in his heart, mind and life since then? Only he and your Lordship know the answer to that.

Then he freely vowed: *'To nourish his faith by the study of God's Word and prayer, in private devotion and public worship.'*

My Lord, I can only ask questions. Does he indeed study God's Word? Indeed, does he even read it regularly? Then, does he pray? Day by day, evening by evening, does he really pray to the God he professes to trust? Or do days go by when he forgets even to pray, in spite of his promise? Does he go to bed at night and give no thanks to God, and ask for no blessing on his loved ones or himself?

Does he devote time to private devotions? Time to be still in the presence of the Lord he vowed to serve? Then he vowed to be faithful in public worship. Is he, my Lord? I leave it to his own conscience to answer as to whether, week by week, he is to be seen meeting with the other saints worshipping his Lord and Master.

He also vowed: *'To live a godly life with the help of the Holy Spirit.'* Again I must ask the simple question—*does he?* Does he live a different kind of life from those around him— the decent godless people with whom he comes in contact day by day. Would he claim that he had fulfilled his promise by living a godly life?

Finally, my Lord, he promised: *'To take due part in the work and witness of the Church and to give of his means for its maintenance and extension.'* Is that a promise he has kept? My Lord and the accused alone know the answer to that question. The work of the church is extensive and demanding. Is he among the first to volunteer for anything that needs to be done? Is he ever seeking new things for the church to do and anxious to be involved in such work?

Then, he promised to be a witness for the church and her Lord. Is he? When others see him, do they recognise that he is a follower of the Lord by the things he does and the things he says?

My Lord, the accused stands before you. He freely and willingly made vows and solemn promises. I ask the simple question—has he kept them?

NARRATOR: The whole scene faded into darkness, but glowing through the shadows I saw the face of the Judge. He had a stern face, deeply scarred with ugly marks and his eyes stared at me with piercing intensity. But it was the expression on that face that broke my heart and made tears flow from my eyes. He had a look of anguished disappointment on his face. I had let him down.

Holiness

16 TESTIMONY—'I saw Jesus!'

Jesus was a good man, the only man I ever knew who was truly holy. I know. I saw him, heard him. There are those who accused him of being a friend of drunkards, sinners and wrong-doers of all descriptions. And they said he was no better than the company he kept. But all accusations of him being evil, a child of Satan, were false. He was holy, and taught others to be holy.

Oh, I know some say he tried to do away with the law of Moses. They could not be more wrong, as anyone who heard him speak will know.

Rather than trying to abolish the law, he actually made it much harder. I mean, he didn't tell us to keep to the cold words of the law, but insisted on us keeping its spirit.

I heard him talking that way, and you can read it for yourself in Matthew's account of Jesus' Sermon on the Mount. He said that while we were all priding ourselves in never having committed adultery, anyone who had looked with lust on a woman had already committed adultery in their heart! The law of Moses regarding murder he treated the same way. If we hate our brother, then we have as good as killed him in our hearts!

That wasn't abolishing the law, it was reinforcing it and bringing it home to us all. Maybe we were proud of being good, but who could say he had never committed mental adultery or mental murder?

Do you see what he was doing? He was turning the searchlight of the law into our very hearts! He was showing us, telling us, what true holiness really is. It is not just physically obeying certain laws, or refusing to violate restrictions. The law should apply to our hearts and imaginations. We must be pure in heart, pure in motive, pure even in the areas that only God sees. That was different from our ideas, where it was simply our outward behaviour that was important.

Jesus did not come to abolish the law, but to *fulfil* it. Indeed, he assured us that as long as heaven and earth remained, the law would not disappear. God's law, like his Word, stands eternal in the heavens. And he wants us to keep that law, keep it in our heart, by being holy. In fact he challenged us to be perfect as our Father in heaven is perfect!

Of course, Jesus did not only talk about holiness—he practised what he preached. He was the only man I have ever known who could hate sin and love the sinner. I once saw a woman who was accused of adultery brought before him. 'By the law of Moses she should be stoned,' was the cry of our teachers of the law. Jesus quietly replied, 'Let him without sin cast the first stone.' That shook them. It shook us all! It suddenly made us realise we were sinners sitting in judgement on another's sin! But Jesus did not leave it there. He never condoned sin. He looked at the woman and commanded her, 'Go and sin no more.'

He was holy in all his words and actions. Alone of all humanity he was sinless perfection. Love governed all his actions and deeds, love for his Father who was God. This love for God and his glory enraged him when he saw the holy Temple made into a den of thieves by the greedy money-changers. It was zeal for God's glory, anger at human sin, that governed his actions.

Yes, there can be no doubt, Jesus was holy in thought, word and deed. And he wants us to be holy—not just in the things we do, but in our hearts and minds.

17 TESTIMONY—'Not as others are!'

I suppose I am a Christian, but I don't actually like to use that word. It sounds sort of religious. Mind you, I've certainly lived a Christian life. No one can point the finger at me. I've never done anyone any harm. And I've been a member of the church for years.

In fact I am an elder and proud of it. I've never missed a communion, if I could help it. I've always delivered the communion cards, even if I've just put them through the letter box when I was in a hurry. But then I've always been a busy man.

I'm keen on golf, bowls and like going to the football. No harm in these things, of course. I know some are not pleased when my golf club competitions are on a Sunday. But it doesn't trouble me. If you're a member of a club you've got to abide by the rules. But I always go to church when there's nothing else on.

No one can say I haven't done my bit for the church. I used to help with the Boy's Brigade when I was younger. And I even helped out one time with the Sunday school.

Now that I'm at the age for retiring, I'm going to take it easy. I think I've earned it. I've done my share. It's someone else's turn. Let the young take over. I'm looking forward to retirement. I will have a good pension, plus a lump sum of money coming to me. So I'll be able to go on a world cruise, take holidays when I like. In fact I'll be able to eat, drink, and take things easy. I think there is something in the Bible about a man like that—a farmer who had a bumper crop and decided to build bigger barns and enjoy the rest of his life with his good luck. I can't remember how the story ended, but I'm going to take things easy now.

(*cf Luke 12:16-21*)

Bible

18 TESTIMONY—Used Bible

I was bought by an old woman as a present for her grandson's 18th birthday. My new owner is not interested in me. In fact I think he was disappointed. He wanted a camera.

I was thrown into a cupboard which houses all his past hobbies—stamp collecting, fishing rod, Lego. I seemed to lie there for months, if not years. I thought I was destined to be always fresh and new, a book that was never to be read.

But then something happened. One night, quite late, I was pulled out of the cupboard and opened. My young owner lay on top of his bed and read several chapters from John's Gospel. He then put me on his bedside table. The next morning he picked me up, and, after flicking through my pages, read one of my Psalms. That night, before going to sleep, he opened me again, and this time read through part of Mark's Gospel.

Night after night it is the same story. He opens me and avidly reads my pages, usually in the New Testament. But he has established the habit of reading one of the Psalms in the morning before going off to work.

I now go to church—it's quite exciting! He proudly carries me there under his arm, twice each Sunday, morning and evening. There, in church, I am opened and read.

My owner is now following some plan of study when he reads me. He no longer just reads me at random at nights, but is systematically studying me. Sometimes he misses a day, once or twice even two, but he always comes back to me. He has even begun to mark me, underlining different verses that he seems to like.

Rather to my surprise he took me on holiday with him— and read me there. I am only three years old, but my spine is becoming slack, my pages are thumbmarked and dog-eared —but I don't mind a bit. I was made to be read and used. As a Bible, I'm a success!

19 TESTIMONY—Unused Bible

I was bought by an old woman. She wanted me to give to her grand-daughter on her 21st birthday. She was very proud of me when I was given to her. She liked my real leather cover, gold leaf pages and fine print. She proudly showed me to all her family.

That night, before going to bed, she flicked through my pages but did not really read any of me. I was then carefully wrapped in my clear cellophane cover and put back into my slipcase. She put me beside her other books, mainly romance and rock magazines. But I could not help noticing that I was put at the far end of the shelf, where I would not be noticed. Perhaps she did not want her friends to see me.

Occasionally she went to church with her family—when she did, I was taken from the bookshelf and carried to church. I don't know why really—I was just put on the pew board and never opened. I was then taken home and put back at the far end of the shelf.

The minister called to see the family and I was taken down to show her. My leather cover, gold leaf and fine pages were noted. I think she was impressed. Grandmother died. The night she was buried, I was taken out and my owner lay on her bed and opened me. But I don't know why she read

Genesis one, and then just flicked over to some verses in Zechariah. I have much more comforting words than these in my pages—she didn't seem to know where to look.

My owner got married and moved away from the house. I was left behind. It was some time later when my owner's mother was decorating that I was taken out and given back to my owner. I was taken to her new home and put away in a cupboard. I must have been there about two years before I was brought out again.

My owner had had a baby boy, and I was taken to church for the baptismal service. Again I don't know why I was taken. I was never opened, and still kept in my cellophane cover. A week later I was taken out of the cupboard and my owner's marriage and date of her first born entered. I was put back in the cupboard.

Two years later this was repeated. It was a baby girl this time. So another name and date was entered on my front page. She now has four of a family!

The cupboard is my home. Only once have I been taken out this past two years. An old minister visited the house and I was shown as a prized possession. I am now twelve years old. I am still in my slip case, my leather binding still protected by clear cellophane, and my pages pristine fresh. I am as new as the day I came from the printers.

As a Bible, I am a complete failure. I was made to be read —but nobody reads me. I am just considered a useless heirloom that will be passed on.

Thanksgiving

20 DIALOGUE—Why be thankful?

ONE: Isn't it a lovely day? Makes you glad to be alive.

TWO: I'm glad you think so!

ONE: Don't you feel like counting your blessings? Being thankful?

TWO: What have I got to be thankful for?

ONE: Well, you're alive, aren't you?

TWO: It's only an existence nowadays.

ONE: But you're alive. You can *see*. Look around you at the lovely world. You can *talk*—even if it's just to tell me your miseries. Think how more miserable you would be if you couldn't moan about it? And you can *hear*—isn't it great to hear little children laughing and birds singing?

TWO: Don't talk to me about birds. They woke me up at four o'clock this morning with all their whistling and screeching.

ONE: At least they're glad to be alive! Maybe we should learn from them—greeting each other with a song!

TWO: I can imagine what my wife would say if I started singing at four in the morning!

ONE: That's something else to be thankful for. You have a wife, a family, a home. They are real gifts from God, you know.

TWO: What is?

ONE: A family! The Bible tells us that God has set the lonely in families. Wouldn't it be a miserable life if we all lived alone in empty houses?

TWO: Sometimes it would be nice to get some peace and quiet.

ONE: And never have anyone to talk to?

TWO: Why are you trying to make out life is so wonderful?

ONE: Because it is! We have comfortable homes, wives, sons and daughters, enough to eat and drink. In fact, it would be interesting to list all the good things we have.

TWO: I don't know. I mean, if you read the newspapers you don't find much to be thankful for.

ONE: Why not give up the newspapers for a day or two. Read the Bible instead.

TWO: The Bible?

ONE: That's full of good news. God loves us, cares for us. He has promised, if we trust him, to be with us all the time—in good days and bad.

TWO: Aha!—so you admit there are bad days!

142

ONE: Of course there are. But, looking back, I know that the bad days with God are better than the good days without him.

TWO: Anyway, I'm not a religious man.

ONE: What's religion to do with it? All I'm saying is that if you like books, the Bible is a good book, the best of all. You should read it if you want good news.

TWO: I like a good book. But have you been to the library lately? It's full of rubbish. Nothing worth reading.

ONE: How about the church? Why not come to church and hear some good news and be thankful.

TWO: I go to church—well, sometimes.

ONE: But don't you hear there about how God loves you; Jesus died for you; and his Spirit will comfort and guide you? Isn't that something to be thankful for?

TWO: You don't know much about me—I don't really have much to be thankful for.

ONE: Come on—*you're alive!* The sun is shining. You have enough to eat, you've never gone hungry, you've three delightful children, a loving wife. You have a God who loves you. And you tell me you have nothing to be thankful for?

TWO: Aye, well, maybe I have—and, then again, maybe I haven't.

Lifestyle

21 INTERVIEW—'I heard Jesus!'

NARRATOR: 'Lifestyle' is a common word today. What sort of style of living should we adopt in the late twentieth century. The teachings of Jesus give many pointers as to the sort of people we should be, and the sort of things we should do. Here is a man who heard Jesus preach.

What did Jesus say about the style of living we should adopt?

MAN: We all know the kind of things we like doing. But Jesus turned everything upside down. He rejected the usual ideas of how we think we should live, and told us to do the opposite. It was mind blowing just to hear him.

NARRATOR: Could you give us an idea of what you mean?

MAN: Well, you know how it is. You look like a man of the world. To get on and live a happy life you need to be rich and carefree, happy and strong, ambitious and ruthless.

NARRATOR: Yes, I suppose some of those characteristics are necessary to live and achieve our ambitions.

MAN: Jesus said no! He told us, if you want to be happy and successful, you must be poor in spirit, mourn for your sins, hunger for the right, be merciful and pure in heart, be a peacemaker. He gave standards totally different from what we might think.

NARRATOR: But all that seems impossible.

MAN: But that was only the start. He spoke about the law.

NARRATOR: Yes, I would expect that. We need the law if we are to have any hope of a civilised society. He emphasised keeping the law, did he?

MAN: Emphasised keeping the law? I'll say he did! I mean, we all thought we were good, never did wrong and kept the law. But Jesus said the law is not just a matter of doing certain things. It's a matter of the heart. We might not commit adultery or murder; but if we have lust or murder in our heart, then we have already broken the law. It's what's in our heart that is important, not what our hands do.

NARRATOR: I've never heard that sort of thing before? What sort of reaction did that create?

MAN: Well, he certainly left us feeling guilty.

NARRATOR: But what about our relationships with others, especially our enemies? Did he say anything about them?

MAN: Yes, he said something about that. No more eye for eye, or tooth for tooth—instead, love your enemies. If someone hits you on the right cheek, then turn the other one.

NARRATOR: But that's impossible! How can anyone act that way?

MAN: I'm only telling you what he said. I know they talk about Jesus as just being another harmless moral teacher —but I tell you he's a real revolutionary.

NARRATOR: I think I'm beginning to see that. What else did he say?

MAN: Things like giving to the needy. But he suggested we should do it secretly, not making a show about it. It was the same with prayer, he said. Do it all in secret.

NARRATOR: But what good is all that? I mean what good is giving and praying if nobody knows you're doing it?

MAN: But somebody does, said Jesus. He told us, 'Your Father in heaven will see and reward you openly.'

NARRATOR: Oh, it's all right giving, but we've got to look after ourselves and our families. Charity begins at home.

MAN: Jesus didn't say that. He told us not to worry or fret about getting on, or getting money in this world. 'Lay up treasures for yourself in heaven,' he said. I suppose he was meaning the giving and praying you should do in secret.

NARRATOR: I cannot see how anyone can live that way.

MAN: But the great thing is we don't need to worry. That's what Jesus said. If God made the flowers so lovely, if he cares for the birds, then surely he cares for us.

NARRATOR: But how does he expect us to live a lifestyle like that? It's impossible!

MAN: He told us to seek his kingdom and his righteousness and all our worries would vanish.

146

NARRATOR: Does he really expect everyone to live the sort of life he preached about?

MAN: No, I'm sure he doesn't. He said there are only two ways, one broad and easy, the other narrow and hard. The broad road leads to destruction and is crowded. Only a few walk the narrow way. I must say, I want to walk in his narrow way. Wouldn't it be great if we all walked in his way?

22 TESTIMONY—'Simple Living!'

We hear a lot of talk today about the need for a simple life-style. At heart I really believe in a simple lifestyle. But, of course, that does not mean doing without things. In fact it means the opposite.

That is why, in our kitchen, we have the latest automatic washing machine, dishwasher, microwave, and a new computerised food-mixer. We have got to take advantage of the latest labour saving appliances. They all make life very much simpler.

We must move with the times. There is no value in being old-fashioned. Naturally, we have a colour television and video recorder. This makes life simpler because we can record programmes we want to see while we're out. We also have televisions for the children—we can't expect them to watch the same programmes that we enjoy. This of course makes family life more simple and harmonious. There are no fights over which programmes to watch.

Our daughter is getting married soon and I have been

thinking about buying a video camera to record the event. It seems simpler to buy one, rather than hire one for the day.

Our son, who's seventeen soon, would like a car. Perhaps it would be simpler just to buy him one, than to have him continually borrowing mine, or my wife's. So, in the interest of a simpler family life, we will probably help him buy a small car.

I think we can be proud of our son and daughter. Certainly we have never denied them anything. We found it much simpler to give them what they want. So they will have a good start in life.

I know all this may appear to make us rather self-centred. But we take our responsibilities seriously. Not, of course, that we *are* selfish. Personally I never pass a flag-seller without giving something, no matter what charity it is. And I once sent a small cheque for some disaster somewhere—I can't remember if it was an earthquake or famine—it was something like that. And we go to church three or four times a year—I always put a pound in the offering plate. So our simple lifestyle has not dried up the charity in our hearts.

Yes, I believe in the simple lifestyle.

(*Suggestion:* Read the story of the Widow's Mite
in *Mark 12:41-44*)

23 AN HONEST PRAYER—
(*Psalm 23*)

Eternal God and Loving Father:

The Lord's my shepherd ...

Lord, I love that Psalm, my favourite among all the hymns we sing in church. Indeed, it is the only one I can sing without the hymnbook. It touches my heart, almost brings tears to my eyes, with its quiet assurance and comfort. And yet, Lord, when I sing that well-known Psalm, I sometimes fear that I get so caught up in the beauty of the poetry and the rhythm of the music, I hardly think of the words at all. I wonder if I really *mean* them, really *believe* them.

The Lord's my shepherd, I'll not want ...

Is that really true? If I am honest, surely I do want lots of things. At times my life seems to be made up of so many desires that are quite unrelated to you. I desire things for myself—success, pleasure, wealth, security. Lord, help me to seek these in you.

In pastures green he leadeth me
The quiet waters by ...

Lord you lead—but do I really follow? Do I really want to follow you? How often I want to go my own way, make my own path through life, without any reference to you! How often I want my ambitions, my hopes to be fulfilled, rather than go the way you would lead.

My soul he doth restore again;
and me to walk doth make
within the paths of righteousness
Even for his own Name's sake ...

Lord, you want to lead me in the paths of righteousness. But often I do not walk there. I sing the words heartily, but in daily living, rather than walking in the righteous way, I go my *own* way. I walk the paths of envy, jealousy, selfishness, greed.

Yea, though I walk in death's dark vale
Yet will I fear none ill ...

Lord, I sing the words, but do I mean them? The truth is I do fear. I worry and fret over many things—my health, my family, the world, the future. You have told me, time after time, not to be afraid. But I am afraid. Afraid of so many things in life and, truth to tell, afraid of death itself.

My table thou hast furnished
In presence of my foes ...

Lord, I know that is true. Day after day you provide me with all that I need. I have never gone hungry. And yet, day by day, sitting down to enjoy the food you have provided—I rarely, if ever, give thanks. You are the good shepherd, caring for me—and I do not give thanks! You lead me in spite of my wanderings.

Goodness and mercy all my life
Shall surely follow me;
And in God's house for evermore
My dwelling place shall be ...

Lord, I can only plead that you will always be with me, just as you promise. Lord, may I continue to praise you. Tune my heart and my lips. And Lord, please, let me sing with words I believe and mean.

Amen